CRYSTALS

FOR HEALTH

THIS IS A CARLTON BOOK

Published in 2013 by Carlton Books Limited
20 Mortimer Street
London W1T 3JW

Originally published in 2010 as part of *The New Crystal Bible*

10 9 8 7 6 5 4 3 2 1

A CIP catalogue record for this book is available from the British Library.

ISBN 978 1 78097 453 8

Printed in China

Disclaimer
The author and publisher shall have no liability or responsibility to any person or entity regarding
any loss or damage incurred, or alleged to have incurred, directly or indirectly, by the information
contained in this book.   The information provided in this book is designed to provide helpful
information on the subjects discussed. This book is not meant to be used, nor should it be used,
to diagnose or treat any medical condition. For diagnosis or treatment of any medical problem,
consult your own physician. The publisher and author are not responsible for any specific health or
allergy needs that may require medical supervision and are not liable for any damages or negative
consequences from any treatment, action, application or preparation, to any person reading or
following the information in this book.

CRYSTALS
FOR HEALTH

Your guide to 100 crystals
and their healing powers

Cassandra Eason

CARLTON
BOOKS

CONTENTS

INTRODUCTION

A book on crystals and gems is like no other book, because it gives access to the fabulous world of nature's most beautiful treasures. Even if you are not a crystal collector, some crystals in the book you may know already or possess as jewellery. Of the 100 minerals in the book, some are relatively rare but are quite magical, while other crystals are not externally dazzling but nevertheless contain healing or restorative properties and become valued like old friends.

Many gems and crystals have acquired myths to explain their perceived properties. Sunstone, the ancients believed, once formed part of the sun and fell to earth during a full solar eclipse. Pearls are said to be tears that fell into the ocean into open oyster shells, the tears of the angels over the sins or sorrows of humankind. This book explains, for each crystal, traditional uses for aiding physical and emotional healing, and also how they can be used practically in the home and to give personal power and protection.

A few of the rarer crystals in their natural form need to be handled carefully because they contain sulphur, lead or other potentially harmful minerals if ingested, but these I have listed. These should be displayed safely away from children or carried wrapped in a small bag.

The book does open the door to the world of wonderful minerals and you may wish to collect your favourites or wear them as jewellery. Even if you do not consider it possible that they have healing powers (and you may change you mind if you try), crystals act as a psychological boost to your energies and self-confidence or give out "do not mess with me" energies that cause others to treat you with more respect. For every crystal works in interaction with the energy field of the user or wearer and so enriches your world every time you use it.

Introducing Crystals

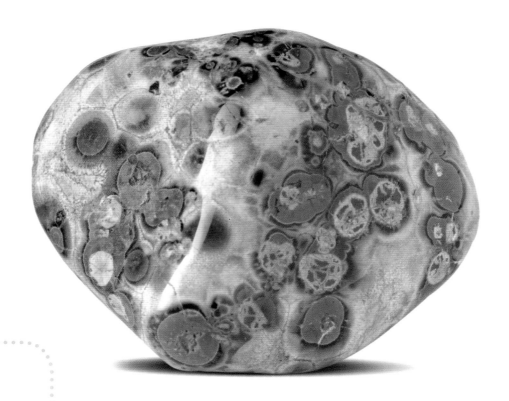

All minerals growing within the Earth have powerful energies, containing the stored natural elemental powers of their formation over millions of years, shaped by volcanic heat and waters seeping deep into the ground. Some, like black obsidian, are not crystals at all but natural glass generated by the sudden cooling of volcano-cascaded lava. Grey or fawn tubes of fulgurite are formed instantly as lightning hits sand. Others are organic, such as pearls, or made of fossils or, like golden amber, from fossilized tree resin, often containing insects or plant material. Green olivine sometimes has extra-terrestrial origins when found in stony and stony iron meteorites.

How a crystal or gem is cut can bring out its true nature. The lustrous moving cat's-eye formation that appears in such gems as yellow chrysoberyl or green alexandrite needs to be skilfully cut into dome-shaped cabochons to display its effect. So do gems that contain a six- or twelve-rayed star, like ruby or sapphire or flash opal with its appearing and disappearing flickers of rainbow colour.

Jewellery is one of the most popular ways to display gems and crystals, and benefit from their healing and empowering qualities directly through skin contact. Traditionally, earrings protect the mind from psychological attack; necklaces and pendants shield the heart from emotional manipulation and bring love; bracelets or arm bands reach out to attract abundance and opportunities. Belt buckles guard and empower the Solar Plexus and Sacral energy centres of the body that control will-power, self-confidence, needs and desires. Rings on any finger symbolize lasting love, friendship and health continuing in a never-ending cycle.

Anniversary stones and birthstones are ways of using polished and often faceted gems as tokens of deep affection or, if bought for oneself, of self-value, and are invariably luck-attracting. Tumbled or tumblestones are a relatively inexpensive way to collect a variety of stones and can be used as worry stones, displayed around the home or even used for divination. Geodes of purple amethyst or yellow citrine with numerous tiny, glittering crystals packed inside are natural ornaments, as are large pieces of dendritic limestone as nature's own unique abstract paintings. Carvings of animals or statues appear in many different stones, from creamy soapstone to deep green verdite, and act as power symbols of qualities we wish to attract, such as the courage of the lion or the focus of the hawk.

How crystals work

Many people find they are instinctively drawn to a particular rock, crystal or gemstone. Some discover that they can physically feel the crystal vibrating with energy; a tingling sensation is experienced whilst holding it. Others find that a crystal or combination of crystals makes them feel better or assists the healing of an ailment. This could be the result to some degree of the placebo effect, the mind and the power of positive thinking healing the body. Alternatively, it could be possible that the crystal's energy vibration is having a physical effect on our bodies, balancing and realigning atoms within our own bodily make-up. Whatever the answer, and there are undoubtedly many more theories,
we do know that thousands of years of history show a proven and undeniable track record of the powerful properties of crystals.

What do the scientists tell us?

Solids (as well as gas and liquid) are made up of atoms, molecules and/or ions. These particles possess energy. They move in all three states – gas, liquid or solid – but differently. In gas they freely and randomly move about and have no particular connection with other particles, and have no regular form. In liquid they are more compressed; they have a "relationship" with neighbouring particles, but still have a certain amount of freedom and space to move about easily – this gives liquid its "flow". Solids are made of particles that are closely compacted together in a regular formation. However, they do have a small amount of space around them, not enough to push or shove past a neighbouring particle, but just enough to allow for a tiny amount of movement, which can cause a vibration, albeit imperceptible to the average human being. Crystals do vibrate, as can all solids.

We all know that quartz has been used to power wristwatches. Quartz is piezoelectric. This means it is capable of generating an electrical charge when under stress. Quartz is commonly used today as a crystal oscillator – an electronic circuit utilizing the mechanical resonance of a vibrating piezoelectric crystal. So, we now know that crystals, at least some of them, have a definite measurable energy.

The huge energy input in the creation of crystals transforms into power for spirituality and healing. Deep within the earth's surface the melting pot of the unknown gives rise to crystals of immense beauty and powerful grounding energies. A collision of material from outer space leaves us its rare and wonderful offspring.

Holding one of these gifts of nature, allowing it to resonate with our own energies and letting it assist us in our healing efforts, whether for our own benefit or to heal another, suggests that crystals have powers, even if these simply mean triggering our own inner healing abilities.

The art of using crystals in healing has developed over many centuries. One day, science may be able to give us a definitive answer as to how and why they work as an aid to healing. Thousands, if not millions, of people have enjoyed the healing benefits of crystals over the centuries and continue to do so today. If they did not work, people would not continue to use them; perhaps this is a good enough reason to believe in what may seem to sceptics to be unbelievable.

CRYSTAL SHAPES AND TERMS

To identify crystals, we look at their mineral content and their structure. Crystals form in a variety of ways and their resulting structures or "habits" can be grouped into six (or sometimes seven) groups or "systems". Crystals are grouped based on the symmetry (or lack of it) of their three-dimensional structures:

Cubic or isometric
This is the simplest and one of the most common crystal forms, where its three axes meet at 90° angles and all are the same length. There are six faces in parallel pairs. This crystal formation has total symmetry. Within the isometric system however, there are 14 more formations, increasing in complexity, built upon this simple structure, for example the dodecahedron and octahedron.
Examples: diamond, garnet and halite, among many others.

Tetragonal
Similar to the cubic (or isometric) system, this has three axes that are at a 90° angle to each other. However, whilst the two horizontal axes are of the same length, the vertical axis is either longer or shorter. Again, there are various formations based on this system, many of which, to the untrained eye, have little resemblance to the simple shape illustrated here.
Examples: scapolite, vesuvianite and zircon.

Hexagonal
In this system there is an additional axis, which gives the crystal six sides. The three horizontal axes meet at 60° angles to each other and the vertical axis is at a 90° angle to the horizontal axes. Included in the hexagonal system is a sub-system called the trigonal system.
Examples of hexagonal: aquamarine, beryl, emerald and zincite.
Examples of trigonal: quartz, ruby, sapphire and tiger's eye.

Orthorhombic
Here, like the isometric system, the three axes meet at a 90° angle to each other, but they are all different lengths.
Examples: chrysoberyl, peridot, sulphur and topaz.

Monoclinic
In this system all the axes have different lengths as with the orthorhombic system, but with two sides perpendicular and the base at an angle, forming a parallelogram.
Examples: azurite, gypsum, jadeite and malachite.

Triclinic
This crystal system has no symmetry. All axes are different lengths and there are no axial angles of 90°.
Examples: kyanite, labradorite, oligoclase and turquoise.

Finally we have amorphous materials. These are not minerals. They are non-crystalline materials but are usually included within the general subject of crystals and gems. Formed by a variety of natural processes such as volcanic activity or fossilization, they include amber, glass, jet, obsidian and opal.

CRYSTALS AND COLOURS

The colour of a crystal is the most important and easiest way of identifying the right one. If a colour is hot like red, associated with life blood and fire, its action will be fast. In contrast, a green crystal represents gradual growth and nature. The shade of a crystal also offers clues: sparkling transparent clear quartz, reflecting sunlight, has different energies from cloudier shimmering white selenite that resembles moonlight. You can enhance the power of a crystal by burning a candle of a similar colour. It is a good idea to build up a collection of crystals in different shades and intensity of brightness. You can also use an antidote colour, for example a blue crystal if someone is very angry or a situation is too fast moving. The following are traditional colour associations.

White colourless
Originality, beginnings, clarity, inspiration, developing talents, ambitions, breaking bad luck, good health, vitality, spiritual development, contact with angels and spirit guides. Can be substituted for any other colour.
Healing powers: May help whole-body healing, general health, integration of mind, body and soul, brain, neurological disorders, auto-immune system, pain relief. **Antidote:** Grey.

White cloudy
(translucent) or opaque (solid colour)
Nurturing, slower new beginnings, especially after loss, slower unfolding potential, protection against negativity, mothers and babies, hope, granting wishes and fulfilling dreams, calling love from the past or afar.
Healing powers: Believed to assist with hormones, fluid balance, fertility, pregnancy, recovery from illness, depression or exhaustion, bone marrow, cells. **Antidote:** Yellow.

Red
Courage, positive change, strength, determination, power, sexual passion, male potency, initiative, competitiveness, protecting loved ones, survival, overcoming obstacles.
Healing powers: Claimed to help improve energy, muscles, low blood pressure, circulation, blood ailments, feet, hands, skeleton, reproductive organs, lifts depression. **Antidote:** Blue.

Orange
Confidence, joy, creativity, female fertility (also red), abundance, independence, self-esteem.
Healing powers: Thought to be good for ovaries, intestines, increases pulse rate, kidneys, bladder, menstruation, menopause, food allergies and addictions, arthritis, rheumatism, immune system **Antidote:** Indigo.

Yellow
Logic, memory, determination, tests, technology, job changes, communication, money-making, short-distance moves and holidays, conventional healing, surgery, repelling malice.
Healing powers: Melp help the lymphatic system, metabolism, blood sugar (also green and blue), digestion, liver, gall bladder, pancreas, spleen, nervous system, eczema, skin problems, nausea, sickness. **Antidote:** Violet.

Green
Love, commitment, beauty, environment, healing via nature, crystal healing, gradual increase of health, wealth, luck.
Healing powers: Thought to be beneficial for heart, lungs, respiratory system, infections and viruses, high blood pressure (also blue), pollen and fur allergies, addictions and obsessions (also blue). **Antidote:** None needed.

Blue

Idealism, justice, career, authority, long-distance travel and house moves, marriage, partnerships, prosperity, peace.
Healing powers: Believed to help thyroid gland, throat, fevers, teeth, cuts, inflammation, childhood rashes, bruises, burns, high blood pressure, eyesight, communication disorders. **Antidote:** Red.

Purple

Spirituality, imagination, dreams, psychic powers, intuition, teaching, counselling, healing from higher sources, banishing past sorrow or present troublesome influences.
Healing powers: Claimed to help with headaches, migraines, scalp, ears, hair, sinusitis, childbirth, addictions, neuroses, phobias, nerve endings and connections, allergies to chemicals and modern living, hyperactivity, insomnia. **Antidote:** Orange.

Pink

Reconciliation, happy family relationships, friendship, kindness, children and teenagers, girls entering puberty, young or new love and trust after betrayal.
Healing powers: Believed to assist with glands, ears, stress headaches, PMS, skin, ulcers, psychosomatic and stress-induced ills, insomnia, nightmares, family ills, children, abuse and self hatred **Antidote:** Dark blue.

Brown

Practical matters, security, accumulation of money, learning new skills in later years, property, finding what is lost, perseverance.
Healing powers: Claimed to be helpful for feet, legs, bowels, hernia, anus, prostate, chronic conditions, growths, degenerative conditons in old age, panic. **Antidote:** Green.

Grey

Adaptability, neutralizing unfriendly energies, peace-making, keeping secrets, shielding from psychic attack.
Healing powers: May help to ease tesions, wounds, burns, tissue and nerve connections, obsessions and acute anxiety, persistent pain. **Antidote:** Clear white.

Gold

Protection, fulfilling ambitions, large infusion of money and resources, long life, recognition, recovery after setbacks, healing when prognosis is not good.
Healing powers: Believed to be beneficial for nervous system, spine, skin, addictions, obsessions and compulsions, minor miracles, healing whole system. **Antidote:** None needed.

Silver

Establishing natural fertility cycles, luck, truth, intuition, female spirituality, unexpected money, attracting love.
Healing powers: May help cleanse toxins, visual disturbances, epilepsy, nightmares, eases passing of a loved one.
Antidote: None needed.

Black

Transformation, peaceful endings, grief, banishing sorrow, guilt and destructive influences, acceptance, blocking a negative force, psychic protection.
Healing powers: Said to assist with pain relief, constipation, IBS, side effects of invasive treatments.
Antidote: Clear white.

CHOOSING & CLEANSING CRYSTALS

Our ancestors looked on hillsides or seashores to find their crystals, and it is still possible to find beautiful stones in nature. Working with crystals local to your area is especially powerful, however, in the modern world there is a huge array of beautifully polished crystals obtainable by anyone. If you want to collect crystals there is no substitute for visiting a specialist crystal store and passing your hand over a tray of similar crystals to feel the one that is right for you. Equally, handling a series of crystal pendulums or gazing within different spheres will reveal which is your special crystal.

At a mineral store, too, you can receive advice about the composition of crystals. Museums with a geological section are usually a good place to buy high-quality mineral specimens. You can also buy crystals by mail order using the images on the Internet site as a guide. Run your hand in front of the screen or over a printout until you feel your palm tingling.

With crystals, size is not important: what matters is the composition of the crystal. Nor should you feel that you need spend a fortune. It is better to buy, for example, a small piece of natural citrine rather than a much larger, heat-treated specimen. Likewise, less colourful stones are preferable to ones that have been dyed. If in doubt check with images on a mineralogical site to see the raw product.

There are a number of ways you can cleanse crystals when you first acquire them, before and after a healing session or if you are using a crystal for good luck or protection. Some methods take a minute or two, but use one of the slower acting techniques at least monthly. If your crystals appear dull or feel heavier than usual they may need extra cleansing.

Water
Wash crystals under a running tap. This works for most tumblestones except those that are fragile or metallic but not for gems. Lapis lazuli and turquoise can be damaged by prolonged water contact. Leave crystals to dry naturally or use a soft cloth kept only for your crystals.

Amethyst geodes
You only need a small amethyst geode (clusters of tiny amethysts embedded in a piece of rock). Stand individual crystals or points on the flat part of the geode. Alternatively make a circle of crystals around a large unpolished amethyst.

The cleansing will take 24 hours. Citrine can be kept with crystals to keep it fresh between more formal cleansing.

Using Mother Earth

Burying crystals in soil for 24 hours is a good way of resting an overworked crystal and is especially effective for crystal points. Choose a deep indoor or outdoor plant pot with a growing plant such as lavender, rose or rosemary or sage herbs. This works best for unpolished natural stones. For a delicate crystal, rest it on top of the soil in an open dish.

Using fragrance

This is suitable for any crystal or gem. Circle a sagebrush or cedar smudge stick or a lemon-grass, pine, juniper, frankincense, lavender or rose incense stick in anti-clockwise spirals over any crystals to be cleansed for three or four minutes. Leave the incense to burn through near the crystals.

Using sound

Collect any crystals to be purified and over them ring either a hand bell or Tibetan bells nine times or strike a small singing bowl over them for about a minute until the sound ceases. Repeat twice more. Sound is an efficient cleanser if you have been working with any intense sorrow or healing when the official medical prognosis of the patient is not good.

Light

Sunlight is the best cleanser for vibrant, richly coloured or sparkling crystals. Leave the crystals from dawn till noon. If the day is cloudy substitute a small gold-coloured or natural beeswax candle for sunlight and leave your crystals in a circle round the candle in a safe place until the candle burns through or goes out naturally. Aventurine, amethyst, aquamarine, beryl, citrine, fluorite and rose quartz do not respond well to sunlight. Crystals in transparent or translucent softer shades or that have clouds or inclusions tend to do better in moonlight, and rose quartz and amethyst are very responsive to lunar energies. The night of the full moon is best for cleansing. Leave all your crystals if possible in a sheltered place outdoors or on an indoor window ledge every month all night on full moon night or a night leading up to the full moon.

Salt

Salt is abrasive and can damage crystals so don't soak the crystals in salt but make three clockwise circles of salt around the crystals. Leave the crystals within the salt circles for about 12 hours, any time of the day or evening and night. Then scoop up the salt from the circles and dissolve it in water. Tip the salt water away under a running tap. Alternatively rest the crystals in a dish on top of a large bowl of salt for 12 hours.

Infusions

This is a very traditional method. Sprinkle a crystal with a few drops of hyssop or rosemary infusion and then wipe it clean with a cloth. To make the infusion, add a teaspoon of dried hyssop or rosemary herb to a cup of boiling water, stir, cover, leave for ten minutes, then strain. Alternatively, use amethyst elixir: soak an amethyst in cold water for a few hours then remove the amethyst. If working with a gem or delicate crystal, sprinkle the infusion round the crystal in circles or float it in a small sealed container in the water or infusion overnight. Dried herbs, particularly sage, thyme, rosemary and hyssop, are excellent cleansers and you can place a delicate crystal or gem in a dish in a larger bowl of herbs for 12 hours.

CRYSTAL HEALING

In addition to being beautiful, crystals can be used to assist in healing the body, mind and spirit. In the sections in this chapter on chakras, auras and crystal healing layouts, I suggest ways you can heal yourself, friends and family or begin more formal healing practices. But crystal healing can be much more spontaneous and informal, and even a beginner can heal themselves or loved ones. If you have a headache, for example, you could choose a crystal that helps to tackle it, such as rose quartz. Alternatively, if you are not certain of the source of an illness or pain, use your intuition and a crystal pendulum to select the right crystal. Warm the crystal in your cupped hands to activate your own innate healing powers and press it gently against the point of discomfort or pain, or wherever instinctively your hand guides you. After a minute or two hold the crystal a few centimetres above the spot or, if a more general malaise, pass it slowly over the front of the whole body, feet to head. Healing will pass through to the back. In either case, allow your hand to move the crystal clockwise or anti-clockwise or both in turn, trusting your intuition to direct you. When you sense healing is complete, remove the crystal and cleanse it.

To choose the right crystal for any purpose spread out all the crystals you have in a circle. At first, you may find it easier to use a crystal pendulum to give you external confirmation that the choice of crystals you sense is right, as you may not trust yourself. You can programme your pendulum, if you are unfamiliar with using one, by moving the pendulum in a clockwise circle and saying, "Let this movement always represent yes for me," and then circle the opposite way and say, "Let this represent no."

Hold your pendulum over each crystal in turn and ask it to give you the yes response if it is the right crystal to help to relieve the condition and/or to reduce any related pain or unpleasant symptoms.

You may find one crystal is enough, in which case it will give no response over all the others. If you have two crystals, you can hold one in each hand and pass them in spirals at the same time over the body or relevant place.

If more than two crystals, then sit in the middle of the crystals, making what seems to be a logical crystal layout with them, for example three in a triangle or four in a square.

MAKING A CRYSTAL ELIXIR

What are crystal elixirs?
Crystal-infused elixirs are empowered water that has been filled with the spiritual energy of crystals by soaking a crystal in the water. The infused water acts as a vehicle for vibrations of the crystal which interacts with the person's own energy field.

Making crystal elixirs - direct infusion method
· A rounded tumbled crystal the size of an average coin will infuse a normal-sized glass or bottle of water. However, you can add two crystals, either of the same kind or with different properties, to quantities of water up to 500 or 600ml.
· Work with three small crystals, the same kind or mixed, for up to 100ml. Increase the number of crystals proportionally if you want even bigger quantities.
· Wash the crystal/s under running water.
· Place the crystal/s in the water using tongs. Still mineral or distilled/filtered water is good; tap water is fine for animals, plants and around the home or your workspace.
· Cover the container or put the lid back on.
· Hold the sealed container between your hands, stating the purpose of the elixir. Ask that the elixir be "created for the greatest good and purest purpose to bring the healing/help/protection in the way that is right for the person/circumstances".
· Leave the water and crystal/s in the refrigerator overnight.
· Unless you have made a glass of crystal elixir to drink immediately, pour the water into suitable containers when you wake.
· Remove the crystal/s.

Crystal waters keep their full power for about 24 hours or three days in the refrigerator.

Indirect crystal elixir
Use this method for a very concentrated elixir with a larger number of the same crystal (up to seven crystals) or crystals with complementary powers, for extra protection, healing or if results seem slow. It is also a suitable method to use with one or two crystals if you are concerned about soaking them directly in drinking water; also for safe elixirs with porous, natural (not tumblestones) or delicate crystals or gemstones, but not for toxic ones (see below).
· Half fill a large glass bowl.
· Hold the crystal/s or gem/s in your cupped hands over the water and stating the purpose of the elixir as in method 1.
· Place the crystal/s or gem/s in a small, fully sealable glass container.
· Close the lid and float the small container in the water in the bowl.
· Cover the bowl or put fine mesh across so it cannot become polluted.
· Leave the bowl for a full 24-hour cycle indoors near a window. Fill bottles with the water and use as needed.

Warning
For crystals listed as toxic, the only safe way to make elixirs is placing a glass or jug of water near a toxic crystal in a sealed container for 48 hours. Make sure the crystal does not come into contact with water or glass.

CREATING A CRYSTAL LAYOUT

By using crystals arranged in a regular geometric formation, called a healing grid or layout, you can concentrate and focus healing energies in a way that is more powerful than working with separate crystals. You can work with as few as three crystals or use as many as you wish to create radiating stars or wheels with lines of crystals. The crystals need only be small.

Using round crystals

You will need one set of six rose quartz or purple amethyst crystals for bringing calm and removing pain and illness. Also a second set of either six yellow citrines or clear quartz crystals for energizing and health-restoring. For removing illness and energizing at the same time alternate three energizers with three calming pain-removers. Arrange the crystals, one over the head and one under the feet as the patient lies down, and the others evenly on either side, a few centimetres away from the body. Add or substitute crystals from the problems list. For extra power, place an additional crystal on the body just above the navel. This should be a crystal related to the main problem.

Crystal points and crystal grids

For more dynamic, faster healing, you can create your layout from six or eight crystal points. Again, set a round crystal related to the problem in the centre on the body. In a crystal layout, set the point facing outwards to remove any illness, sorrow, addictions, blockages or pain and pointing inwards to energize and to bring healing. Alternatively, position the points so every other one faces outwards to bring balanced energies. Double-terminated crystals, with a point at both ends, ensure a two-way energy flow. For the simplest procedure, having set up the layout and asked the blessings of angels and guides, sit

or lie within the crystal grid for between 15 and 20 minutes and let nature do its work. Afterwards remove the crystals one by one in reverse order of setting.

The Master crystal

For additional power, join together the individual crystals with what is called a master crystal. In direct healing, this is usually a pointed, thin, clear wand-like crystal. Touch each crystal with the master crystal wand once you have set the crystal in its grid position and then draw visualized lines of light between the crystals moving clockwise to join them to each other. Join these visualized lines of light as if you were drawing them physically, starting and finishing at the highest point over the head and then go round a second or even third time until you feel the vibrating humming connection of the crystals. Finally, touch the central crystal with the wand and picture straight rays of pulsating light radiating from it connecting it to every other crystal. For absent healing, if using a photo, you can set a larger master crystal cluster in the centre and visualize the rays of light forming a wheel with the central crystal as the hub, radiating out to each of the individual crystals.

Healing with a layout

You or the person to be healed should lie flat with the head slightly propped up. For a shorter treatment, arrange the crystals around a chair and ask the patient to hold the central crystal or set it under the middle of the chair. If the grid is on the floor, kneel to join the crystals with the visualized light rays using your wand. If the layout is round yourself you can create the shape in light over your head with the master wand as you visualize the figure of light expanding to enclose you.

CRYSTALS AND CHAKRAS

Chakra power

Chakras are the driving force of our inner energy system, made up of seven main energy centres controlling different parts of the body and mind and energy channels that link them. Chakras are part of our inner spiritual body, described as whirling rainbow vortices of energy that empower the aura, the energy field around us that receives and transmits life force between us and the world.

To feel your chakras, hold the palm of the hand you do not write with over each area. If the chakra is in balance, you will sense a warm swirling sensation. If the sensation feels jarring or unpleasant, the chakra is probably overactive; if you feel nothing, it may be blocked. Each chakra has its own crystals, listed in each entry in the directory.

Chakra 1 Root or Base

Colours: Red, brown, grey and black.

Located in the perineum; can also heal through the thighs and minor related chakras in knees, ankles and soles of the feet.

Key qualities: Physical power, strength, immediate action, the physical self, self-preservation.

Balanced: Good health, stamina, perseverance, developed instincts.

Unbalanced: Flight-or-fight reactions, excessive fear, anger or irritability; locked in routine, blunted instincts, stuck in past sorrows.

Rules: Legs, feet and skeleton including teeth (also Throat chakra), base of spine, bones and joints, bowels, large intestine, anus, prostate gland, testes, penis (also Sacral), basic cell structure.

Move crystals over chakras anti-clockwise for women and clockwise for men.

Chakra 2 Sacral or Hara

Colours: Orange, silver.

Located just below navel and womb.

Key qualities: Sexual desire, pleasure, self-esteem, self-image, independent judgment, connection with others through balanced emotions, ability to accept change.

Balanced: Acceptance of, and pleasure in, basic desires for love, approval, food, gut intuitions about others; balance between dependency and independence.

Unbalanced: Doubting own value, over-reliance on authority figures; orally focused addictions; easily unbalanced by stress.

Rules: Abdomen, lower back, female reproductive system (also Root), blood, all bodily fluids and hormones, menstrual and menopausal problems, kidneys, bladder, innermost child, the person we are inside.

Move crystals over chakra clockwise for women and anti-clockwise for men.

Chakra 3 Solar Plexus

Colours: Yellow.

Located around centre of upper stomach.

Key qualities: Integration of experiences; unfulfilled potential; rejection of what is not helpful; self-confidence; intellectual power.

Balanced: Learn from mistakes and take new

opportunities; apply thought and determination rather than sentiment in decision-making.
Unbalanced: Feeling at the mercy of fate, restless, indecisive; alternatively workaholic tendencies and obsession with worldly success, compulsive behaviour.
Rules: Digestion, liver, spleen, gall bladder, stomach and small intestine, middle back, autonomic nerve system, metabolism.
Move crystals over chakra anti-clockwise for women and clockwise for men

Chakra 4 Heart
Colours: Green and pink.
Located in the centre of the chest; also rules chakras in palms of the hands and fingertips and the minor thymus chakra in upper chest.
Key qualities: Compassion, social identity, appropriate roles for stages of life, self-love, love of and with others, healing powers via hands and arms, healing with herbs and nature, inner harmony, environmental awareness.
Balanced: Giving and receiving love equally; empathizing without drowning in responsibility; valuing self as you are; appreciation of beauty.
Unbalanced: Over-emotional outbursts, sentimentality, possessiveness, jealousy, allergies to plants and animals, panic attacks.
Rules: Upper back, rib cage, chest, lymph glands, skin, circulatory system, lower lungs, abdominal cavity, skin.
Move crystals over chakras clockwise for women and anti-clockwise for men.

Chakra 5 Throat
Colour: Sky or light blue.
Located round the base of the throat and the Adam's apple; also at the base of the brain at the back of your neck as minor Brain-stem chakra.

Key qualities: Clear communication with outer world and within self, creativity, ideas and ideals, concentration, ability to deal with the abstract, speaking the truth with kindness, cultural values, listening as well as talking, dreams and unconscious wisdom.
Balanced: Expression of creativity, personally or professionally, leadership qualities, justice, and fair-mindedness; activates the blueprint of your life plan, the ideal person you can become; healing through crystals.
Unbalanced: Communication difficulties, voice loss or stammering, outbursts of inappropriate language when frustrated, minor dishonesty or illusion, alternatively sarcasm, rigid ideas, prejudice.
Rules: Neck, voice mechanism, bronchial passages, jaw, mouth, eyes, passages to ears.
Move crystals over chakra anti-clockwise for women and clockwise for men.

Chakra 6 Brow or Third Eye
Colour: Indigo (bluish purple) or different shades of purple, tinged with silver.
Located just above the bridge of the nose.
Key qualities: Imagination, clairvoyant and healing powers, ability to communicate with angels and spirit guides, divergent or inspirational thinking; very active chakra in children.
Balanced: Ability to grasp the whole picture, evolved intuition and imagination, higher spiritual healing abilities through angels and guides.
Unbalanced: Problems accepting life as it is, dreaming life away, headaches and inability to cope with pressures of modern life.
Rules: Ears, visual clarity, sinuses, pituitary gland, face, both hemispheres of the brain, radiating into the central cavity of the brain.
Move crystals over chakra clockwise for women and anti-

clockwise for men.

Chakra 7 Crown
Colours: Violet, rich purple merging into pure white and gold.
Located at top of head in the centre where the three main bones of the skull fuse at the anterior fontanelle to several centimetres above the head; merges with higher Soul Star chakra and cosmos.
Key qualities: Integration of mind, body and spirit, prophecy, ability to reach the top in any chosen field, nobility of spirit and actions, seeking perfection; universal energy healing powers such as Reiki.
Balanced: Wisdom, sense of being at home in body, but also able to see beyond the material world; fulfilment of major dreams and ambitions.
Unbalanced: Alienation from life, indefinable recurring mild flu-like illnesses; alternatively obsession with perfection and beauty, leading to inability to value real love or happiness.
Rules: Higher brain functions, skull, auto-immune system, neurological conditions, whole-body health and long life. Move crystals over chakras anti-clockwise (women) or clockwise (men).

Assessing chakra health
Pass the hand you do not write with a few centimetres away from the body over the seven main chakras. You can assess and heal minor chakras via their ruling one. When assessing someone else's chakras you may feel the chakra sensations in your own body or see images in your mind.

Chakra healing with chakra crystals
You can heal blocked or over-active chakras with small round or oval chakra crystals, by holding the appropriate crystal in turn on the relevant area. The body will take the

required amount of healing from each crystal through its chakra. But if any chakra was particularly blocked or in overdrive when you assessed it, you can give it extra input.

Chakra touch healing
Choose a crystal for each chakra; use the hand you write with to hold it. Place your seven chakra crystals on a table nearby. Ask for blessings and guidance from the angels and guides and hold each crystal over the appropriate chakra area in turn, from Root up to Crown. Gently massage the chakra in the direction suggested for each. This will slow down or unblock it. Trust your hand and the crystal. If you do not know the person well, you can hold each crystal a few centimetres away from the body, circling the crystal over the chakra. When you sense the energies are balanced, return the crystal to the table and continue with the next crystal until you have used all seven. If any area seems particularly troublesome, return to the affected chakra with the appropriate crystal. Pass your hands down either side of the body, a few centimetres away from it, to smooth the energies of the aura energy field surrounding the body. Cleanse your pendulum and crystals.

CRYSTALS AND THE AURAS

The aura is a rainbow-coloured energy field that surrounds everything. People have an aura made up of seven bands of coloured light that encloses the individual, extending about an arm span all round. This can be seen externally by those with evolved clairvoyant sight, by children and with the inner eye by almost everyone.

Each of the seven aura layers is related to, and is the same colour as, one of the main seven chakras and so shares the same crystals. Each aura layer, like its chakra, is linked with specific body organs and functions; for everyday crystal work, aura crystals are mainly used for empowerment or protection of the energy field and to cleanse the aura of any negativity.

You will need: a clear crystal pendulum or clear crystal point, 14 aura crystals, two in each of the main seven colours, one in a vibrant shade to energize a sluggish aura colour and one in a gentler tone to slow overactivity.

Assessing the aura by touch

Aura energies become lighter the further away from the body they are. The easiest way to assess the intensity, shade and the smoothness or streakiness of the colours to gain information about the person whose aura you are studying is through psychic touch. This information reveals when the use of a specific aura crystal will help to restore balance in the aura and so in life.

As well as the seven colours of the rainbow that move outwards in order, gold, white and other colours may appear in the aura. These minor colours are attached to the seven main rainbow bands and empowered by a minor chakra. The easiest place to assess the aura is round the head and shoulders and

this is also the best place to empower and seal or protect the aura from stress or negativity. It may be helpful to cleanse and re-empower your aura weekly or more often after a bad day.

Working with the aura
· Begin with your own aura or a friend or close family member so you will feel relaxed.
· Take your clear crystal pendulum or a clear single or double terminated crystal point in the hand you write with; pass it through your aura in a weaving movement starting above your head and going down to your shoulders on either side, including your hair for the innermost layer will reach your scalp.
· Pass the pendulum slowly from a central position several centimetres above the crown of your head to find the outermost layer limits of your aura. It will be the same distance approximately all round down to your shoulders.
· You will sense in your fingertips a buzzing where the outer limits of the aura merge into the cosmos. If you cannot detect anything, move your hand slowly inwards as your aura may be temporarily smaller if you are tired, unwell or under pressure.
· Once located, follow this sparkly edge where the aura touches the cosmos round your head and shoulders.
· Once you have found the outermost layer, move your pendulum inwards in small spirals, assessing how the layer feels. Did it feel too powerful, like putting your hands in very fast-moving water? Did you detect any faded areas where the energy disappeared or a spot where the energy appeared tangled? These are places to return with your relevant aura crystal.

THE CRYSTAL DIRECTORY

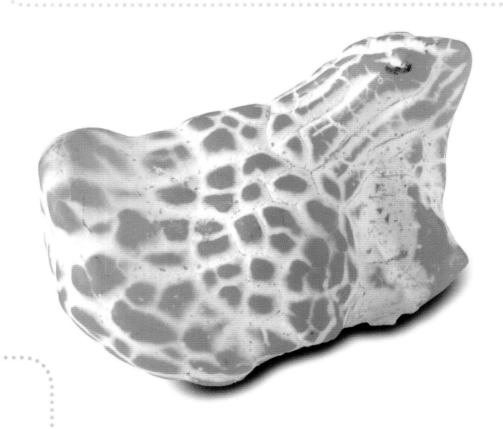

The 100 crystals are listed according to colour so that you can easily find ones for particular purposes. I have given the overall colour meanings on pages 10–11 for fast reference. Colour is a good indication of the basic nature of the crystal. For example red crystals and gems tend to be far more dynamic in their energies and faster acting than more reflective purple ones and more concerned with action in the material world. But within the colour groupings there are variations that partly depend on the chemical composition and partly on the shade or vibrancy of the individual crystal.

Each entry is divided into categories so you can check its individual properties, beginning with the kind of crystal and its physical and emotional healing properties. There are also listings for everyday uses and magical significance which include working with a crystal for spiritual or psychic development, in meditation or in rituals and empowerments. Each is related to a specific chakra and on pages 18–20 is information about the different energy centres of the body and how related chakra crystals can be used to bring the body and mind into harmony. There are particular fragrances you can burn as you meditate or relax. The sign of the zodiac associated with the crystal is given as you may find your personal star sign crystals are particularly lucky or empowering. The divinatory meaning explains the essential quality of the crystal. Finally, a short section of information describes what makes that crystal unique and also sometimes the myths and beliefs that have grown up around it to explain those special qualities.

Rose Quartz

Type: Silicon dioxide: quartz with manganese impurities, sometimes embedded in the form of tiny needles, sometimes crafted or found naturally as heart shapes.

Colours: Pink, translucent, glowing and semitransparent to clear pale or deeper pink; untumbled ice-like chunks of rose quartz are also sold.

Availability: Common.

Physical benefits: Said to help circulation; healing mothers after a complicated birth; skin, especially stress-related conditions; headaches, fertility, genitals, female reproductive system, healthy flow of fluids.

Emotional healing: Depression, especially post-natal depression, forgiving mistakes, your own as well as others; the best crystal for overcoming abuse of all kinds.

Chakra: Heart.

Adonis, lover of the Greek goddess Aphrodite (Venus in Roman lore), was attacked by the god Ares disguised as a boar. Rushing to save him, Aphrodite caught herself on a briar bush. Their blood stained the quartz pink. This crystal helps you mother yourself. During pregnancy, hold it on your stomach to form a bond with your child. It will also soothe you after birth. Called the heart stone, rose quartz may have been a love token as early as 600 BC.

Place twin rose quartz hearts with pink roses on a love altar and light pink candles nightly to call love or strengthen a relationship. Alternatively, enclose a photo of yourself and a lover with tiny rose quartz crystals in a heart shape.

Candle colour: *Pink.*

Fragrances: *Lemon balm, lemon verbena, lilac, lily of the valley, rose and ylang ylang.*

Practical uses: *The best sleep crystal for adults and children: prevents nightmares, night terrors and will bring beautiful dreams. It helps children not to be afraid of the dark.*

Magical significance: *Rose quartz is the crystal of reconciliation. Cast a tiny one in flowing water at sunset and speak words you would like to say.*

Divinatory meaning: *Forgive yourself for past mistakes and do not accept the blame others try to offload for their inadequacies. If someone cannot accept the real you, that is their problem.*

Zodiac: *Taurus.*

Empowerment: *I will be as kind to myself as I am to others.*

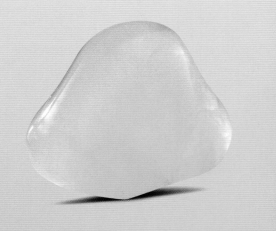

PINK DANBURITE

Type: Calcium borosilicate.

Colours: Very pale pink and like clear glass (also occasionally yellow, grey or brown).

Availability: Rarer than colourless danburite in all its forms.

Physical benefits: May help heart, heart bypasses and transplants, muscle weakness; even gentler than clear danburite for the young, infirm and very sick animals or birds, particularly small or injured ones; may ease allergies or illnesses aggravated by the fast pace of the world.

Emotional healing: For victim support, for hijack victims or those who have witnessed major disasters

Chakra: Heart

Danburite is a recent discovery, cast up by Mother Earth about the time of the Industrial Revolution to heal ills caused by the frantic pace of modernity; the rarer pink danburite addresses the needs of people forgotten by society; good for anyone caught up in an acrimonious divorce, to feel safe. Danburite clusters in an infant's room soothe a little one who wakes crying in the night. If a partner or close family member is manipulating in the name of love, pink danburite, worn over a period, will bring quiet strength to break free.

Candle colour: *Deep pink.*
Fragrances: *Apple blossom, rose, violet.*
Practical uses: *Pink danburite helps children to play together.*
Magical significance: *Pink danburite calls healing powers from angelic sources; a piece of pink danburite can form the centre of a healing grid with six pieces put around a patient's head, feet, elbows and knees.*
Divinatory meaning: *You discover why a friend has been out of touch and may need to offer support.*
Zodiac: *Taurus and Aquarius.*
Empowerment: *Gentleness is not a sign of weakness but inner strength.*

PINK TOURMALINE

Type: Silicate.

Colours: Pink.

Availability: Common.

Physical benefits: Seen as helpful for spinal problems or injuries, the nervous system, neuralgia and migraines; for boys and girls approaching puberty; all gynaecological conditions, especially to regularize the menstrual cycle to make conception easier.

Emotional healing: Reduces fear and panic; the best crystal for teenage pregnancy and to assist in bonding with baby.

Chakra: Heart and Crown.

Egyptian legend speaks of how tourmaline made its journey from the centre of the Earth and passed over a rainbow, taking with it all of the colours as its own. Pink came from the early-morning sky. Pink tourmaline is one of the most loving stones, comforting children who have suffered from any form of abuse. Take off pink tourmaline jewellery at night so its shielding effects do not shut out positive energies as well as negative if worn 24/7.

Candle colour: *Pink.*
Fragrances: *Anise, lavender.*
Practical uses: *Protective during travel.*
Magical significance: *Use pink tourmaline to call back an estranged lover. Pass through the smoke of a rose incense stick, scatter rose petals round it and sprinkle with rose water, saying, "Through sky, by earth, through fire and across water, may my love not hesitate to return".*
Divinatory meaning: *Your inner child is in need of healing – take time to have fun.*
Zodiac: *Taurus and Scorpio.*
Empowerment: *I welcome and offer love and kindness.*

MORGANITE

Type: Cyclosilicate/beryl.

Colours: Pink, rose-lilac, peach, orange or pinkish yellow, sometimes with colour banding; coloured by manganese and lithium.

Availability: Obtainable from specialist jewellers, crystal stores and online.

Physical benefits: May help larynx, tongue, thyroid gland, lungs and nervous system, heart palpitations and irregularities, burns and scalds.

Emotional healing: For girls entering puberty who do not have a mother and for younger women struggling with eating disorders.

Chakra: Heart.

Called after its discoverer, John Pierpont Morgan, an American banker who was interested in magic and mineralogy, morganite has been adopted as a stone for lawyers to ensure fairness. Use morganite to show compassion towards people who may have mental or emotional problems or physical illnesses that make them hostile towards others. Wearing morganite for a few weeks helps express emotional needs you have considered unreasonable, but which are necessary to make a relationship more equal. Also known as Pink Beryl.

Candle colour: *Pink.*
Fragrances: *Apple blossom, lavender, lemon balm, rose.*
Practical uses: *Take a piece to meetings with bank managers and accountants to ensure you get fair treatment.*
Magical significance: *Opens communication with your guardian angel.*
Divinatory meaning: *You may feel a very small fish in a very big pool, but you can speak out over a matter where you know you are right.*
Zodiac: *Taurus.*
Empowerment: *I will be slow to prejudge others.*

SUGILITE

Type: Cyclosilicate.

Colours: Pale pink to lavender pink to magenta/fuchsia, streaked with black.

Availability: Pink rarer than in violet/purple.

Physical benefits: Believed to assist with pain relief (especially from burns), infections and viruses, functioning of the adrenal, pineal and pituitary glands, dyslexia, autism, Asperger's syndrome.

Emotional healing: Pink sugilite is a stone of the heart and resolves inner hurt; helpful for adopted children rejected by birth-parents they have tracked down.

Chakra: Heart.

Though not considered as valuable as its rich-purple-coloured sister, pink sugilite, especially in magenta or fuchsia shades, is a powerful love crystal; avoids sentimentality in relationships while encouraging commitment in good times and bad. Wear pink sugilite jewellery to attract a kindred spirit; also encourages a love of life and belief in inherent goodness of people. Pink sugilite brings balance to food-related addictions and compulsions such as excessive alcohol, gambling or out-of-control spending.

Candle colour: *Bright pink.*
Fragrances: *Carnation, hyacinth, lilac, orchid.*
Practical uses: *An excellent crystal for children who find socializing hard.*
Magical significance: *An excellent amulet for children who recall past lives; keeps the balance between everyday practicalities and the spiritual world.*
Divinatory meaning: *Loving someone does not mean you have to accept their bad moods.*
Zodiac: *Taurus and Aquarius.*
Empowerment: *I will not get stuck in self-pity.*

BUSTAMITE

Type: Manganese calcium silicate, sometimes found with sugilite (p.28).

Colours: Predominantly pale to deep pink; also red, brownish red and red-brown.

Availability: Obtainable from specialist crystal stores and online.

Physical benefits: May benefit the heart, especially irregular heartbeat, circulation, keep older people mobile for longer, said to help tumours, melanomas.

Emotional healing: Bustamite is a stone of gentle courage, to give the strength to leave an abusive situation.

Chakra: Heart and Brow.

Candle colour: *Pink.*
Fragrances: *Almond blossom, honey, neroli, peach.*
Practical uses: *Bustamite encourages relaxation and makes any home or workplace welcoming.*
Magical significance: *Brings sanctity to weddings, baby blessings and natural burials.*
Divinatory meaning: *Care for your health and comfort and ask for any support you need, though you may find this hard if you are normally self-sufficient.*
Zodiac: *Taurus.*
Empowerment: *I can put down roots wherever I am.*

This beautiful and sometimes brightly coloured stone brings connections with others and eases relationships at work with people who may be unapproachable; softens cantankerous family members. Bustamite also increases love in new relationships; grounding for anyone who dreams of the perfect lover and gives up at the first hurdle when a relationship runs into difficulties. Bustamite spreads gentle healing and unblocks the entire body's energy centres if placed on a patient's heart or in the centre of the chest or breasts where the Heart chakra energy centre lies.

ANDEAN OPAL

Type: Hydrated silicon dioxide, common opal, displaying no iridescence.

Colours: Pink, pastel-coloured with a pearl-like sheen. Availability: Relatively rare as true Andean opal (some are dyed substitutes).

Physical benefits: May aid healing children, animals, very old or chronically sick people; skin irritation, dryness or cracking, eyesight, heart, low blood sugar, diabetes.

Emotional healing: Very calming for children and adults who are overwhelmed by life; also for timid animals you have adopted.

Chakra: Heart.

A stone to help all to trust again after an attack, abuse or betrayal. Wear pink opal to bring joy into your life if your emotions have become very flat or you feel disengaged. Pink opal is a tough-love stone when life is hard, to prevent sentiment standing in the way of speaking honestly to others if someone is abusing your trust. Good for a reality check in relationships or where one partner is very needy and stifling, to gain emotional completeness and not constantly drag up the past as a weapon to avoid dealing with present issues.

Candle colour: *Pink.*
Fragrances: *Almond, apple blossom, hibiscus, peach, pink rose.*
Practical uses: *If you find it hard to accept help or gifts and are one of life's fixers, pink opal allows you to be more receptive to others' generosity.*
Magical significance: *Pink opal is sacred to Pachamama, the Peruvian earth mother, and considered one of her gifts; wear or carry pink opal to attract love.*
Divinatory meaning: *Kindness from a stranger will restore your faith in life.*
Zodiac: *Taurus.*
Empowerment: *To accept help is not weakness.*

PINK CHALCEDONY

Type: Cryptocrystalline quartz.

Colours: Varying shades of creamy pink. The pink is due to the presence of manganese or ferrous oxide impurities.

Availability: Relatively common.

Physical benefits: Believed to ease ageing, skin and wrinkles, baby and childhood illnesses, especially rashes; pregnancy problems, especially high blood pressure and pre-eclampsia; good for first-time mothers, those who have had surgical intervention and post-natal problems such as scars and stitches not healing or mastitis that makes breast-feeding difficult.

Emotional healing: Helps with compulsion and obsession, including obsessive compulsive disorder, fear of germs; also post-natal depression, abuse especially in early childhood.

Chakra: Heart.

This is a crystal of kindness: a bowl of pink chalcedony, mangano calcite and rose quartz tumblestones will bring gentleness, harmony, and affection to any home.

Give to children who are jealous of a new family member, especially a new baby; also helps animal mothers to care for their young. A goddess stone, pink chalcedony may be worn as a cross by women who seek the feminine aspects of God within conventional religion.

Pink chalcedony worn as jewellery will ease heartache; buy it to mark a new beginning.

Pink chalcedony may help children deal with a family crisis such as divorce or bereavement; good, too, to help a girl love her changing body, especially if puberty comes early.

Candle colour: *Pink.*
Fragrances: *Clary sage, neroli, rose, rosewood, violet.*
Practical uses: *Pink chalcedony is known as the baby stone, given to a woman before birth and set on a mother's stomach to increase communication between her and her child. After the birth it was kept beneath the baby's crib to keep away all harm.*
Magical significance: *A fun stone for releasing or rediscovering your inner child and to connect with the wonders and magic of the natural world, if you have become very serious or weighed down by responsibility.*
Divinatory meaning: *A sudden reminder from the past may temporarily shake you, but you can now deal with buried feelings positively once and for all.*
Zodiac: *Taurus and Pisces.*
Empowerment: *I release old sorrows to make room for joy.*

RHODOCHROSITE

Type: Manganese carbonate.

Colours: Rose pink with white or paler pink banding, though this can vary from lighter pink to almost red, opaque; may also contain orange, yellow and brown. Very occasionally transparent pink crystals can be found.

Availability: Common.

Physical benefits: Thought to help with circulation, heart problems, blood pressure, breathing problems, asthma, stress-related migraines.

Emotional healing: Unblocks psychic chakra energy centres so light and power can flow upwards into the body from the earth via the Root chakra, from the natural world through the Heart chakra and downwards through the Crown from the cosmos; this can help you move towards the future after doubt and express love without fear of rejection.

Chakra: Heart/Solar Plexus.

Rhodochrosite is known as the Inca rose because it was believed to contain the blood of their ancestral rulers.

If you seek news of a lost friend, relative or love, place the crystal next to their photograph: putting your hands on either side of the crystal, say their name softly three times and ask them to get in touch. Visualize the person where and when you last were together. Leave the crystal next to the photograph.

For an animal, put the crystal where the pet used to love sitting. Hold it between your cupped hands and imagine the animal back in its place. Leave the crystal on a surface near the entrance or exit the animal used most.

Candle colour: *Bright pink.*

Fragrances: *Anise, cedarwood, copal, hibiscus, lime, orange, rose, rosewood.*

Practical uses: *Helpful for children starting childcare, school, a new school or college so that they find friends easily and settle in; a good gift to new family members such as step-children.*

Magical significance: *A calling-back crystal, whether a lost lover, friend or relative who has broken off contact or a missing pet.*

Divinatory meaning: *Open your heart to the possibility of love and friendship and you may find that it was close to you or present all the time; choose old valued friends rather than exciting new acquaintances.*

Zodiac: *Sagittarius.*

Empowerment: *I allow love to flow freely to and from my heart and most of all to love and value myself.*

PINK TOPAZ

Type: Fluorine aluminium silicate; occurs naturally but many pink topaz are dyed.

Colours: From pale to brighter or reddish pink. Availability: Rare in untreated form.

Physical benefits: Thought to reduce toxins in body, breasts and ovaries; may help with early-onset puberty, menopause, HRT treatment, inflammation, burns and fevers, fertility, insomnia, asthma, haemmorrages, heart palpitations and weakness, hearing and earache.

Emotional healing: For creating a balance between being open to love and trust, and not giving or loving too much or over-identifying with your partner or would-be lover.

Chakra: Heart

Untreated pink topaz is one of the most valuable forms of topaz and is found in Pakistan and Russia. Oscar Wilde (1854–1900) likened pink topaz to the eyes of a wood pigeon. The first artificial pink topaz was created in 1750, when a Parisian jeweller discovered that yellow topaz turns pink if exposed to moderate heat.

A very hard gem, pink topaz is one of the more powerful pink crystals, representing love and dreams that are realistic, not unattainable; it eases obsessing or wating in hope for an unattainable love.

Like all topaz, the pink form helps uncover falsehoods and illusions; hold it or wear it to enable you to distinguish between groundless fears that love will not last or that you are not good enough for love from what are real doubts about fidelity or intention.

Candle colour: *Pink.*

Fragrances: *Almond blossom, apple blossom, cherry blossom, magnolia, rose.*

Practical uses: *Wear pink topaz to take away sadness if you have been hurt in love, and to heal your sorrow; a wonderful gift to a first love to signify affection that will continue to grow.*

Magical significance: *Brings luck in love. Using the smoke of a rose incense stick or the index finger of the hand you do not write with, write the name of the person you wish to attract or "whoever will make me happy and I him/her". Enclose the smoke or visualized words with a smoke- or air-drawn heart shape.*

Divinatory meaning: *If you have been hurt, go slowly in new love so you feel secure; do not rush into a new commitment.*

Zodiac: *Taurus.*

Empowerment: *I am willing to take a risk and trust again.*

BIXBITE/RED BERYL

Type: Beryl, ring silicate, sometimes called the red emerald.

Colours: Red to pinkish red.

Availability: Rare as gem quality, obtainable in specialist crystal stores and jewellers and online.

Physical benefits: Thought to be good for heart, liver, lungs, mouth, throat, stomach, ulcers of all kinds, chilblains and winter chills, raising and maintaining energy levels; good for the chronically ill or the very old who feel the cold.

Emotional healing: A stone to overcome grief and emotional heartbreak, loss and betrayal, to open the Heart chakra energy centre to future love.

Chakra: Heart.

Bixbite protects against psychic and psychological vampires and against all who would manipulate you. Wear or tape it close to your navel if you know you will be meeting someone whose charms are hard to resist; wear or take it when you make a major purchase to choose wisely and not be swayed by sales talk.

A stone of passion, bixbite will kindle sexual desire if you love but are afraid because of previous bad experiences. A good wedding or pre-wedding gift to remind you why you are marrying. Also a stone of reconciliation if a partner has been unfaithful, to set between you as you talk to find if there is a way back.

Helps heal family estrangement, especially if you argued over a love choice. Also helps to form the right channels to talk to your ex-partner's new love about your children.

Candle colour: *Red.*

Fragrances: *Anise, dragon's blood, hibiscus, poppy, thyme.*

Practical uses: *A crystal of warm, affectionate lasting love; wear or carry bixbite to attract someone with whom you are compatible and to keep a relationship caring and supportive even in bad times.*

Magical significance: *Use in love magic to call your twin soul by holding the bixbite up to candlelight at midnight and asking your other half to find you. Blow out the candle and sleep with bixbite taped close to your heart.*

Divinatory meaning: *You may be tempted to act impulsively and unwisely; consider the consequences carefully.*

Zodiac: *Aries and Taurus*

Empowerment: *I value lasting love and loyalty rather than excitement.*

Poppy Jasper

Type: Silicate, microcrystalline quartz with mineral or organic inclusions.

Colours: Brick red with shades of brown or black, also golden yellows, cream, or white in a single stone; Morgan Hill jasper has red and yellow orbs resembling poppies.

Availability: One of the less common jaspers.

Physical benefits: May help adrenalin regulation, low energy, certain allergies, anaemia, irregular menstruation, summer colds, infectious illnesses with rashes.

Emotional healing: Caffeine addiction, extreme anxiety.

Chakra: Heart.

Wear poppy jasper next to the skin for a regular infusion of happiness and energy; excellent for giving the impetus for a pleasurable, new health regime. Because of the association of poppies with remembrance and peace, poppy jasper makes a good reconciliatory gift or can be set around a map to bring world peace; give tumblestones to friends or family to maintain regular contact.

  Poppy jasper overcomes lethargy and depression. It also helps to encourage consideration and communication around the physically disabled.

Candle colour: *Red.*
Fragrances: *Carnation, geranium, hibiscus, poppy, red rose.*
Practical uses: *The joy bringer, encourages outdoor pursuits and helps to keep plants healthy.*
Magical significance: *Sit near any ancient site or temple holding poppy jasper to connect with the world chakras and become energized and empowered.*
Divinatory meaning: *Enjoy the moment and think about all the good things in your life.*
Zodiac: *Aries.*
Empowerment: *I am happy with my life.*

BLOOD AGATE

Type: Chalcedony, crypto-crystalline quartz; also known as red agate or pigeon's blood.

Colours: Red and white, translucent and glowing, resembles coagulating blood.

Availability: Relatively common.

Physical benefits: May be useful for blood disorders, circulation, excessive bleeding; menstrual problems, hysterectomy, energy and stamina, fertility, digestive and lymphatic systems; one of the best stones for good health.

Emotional healing: A survival stone, when a person has lost the will to live, or harms or neglects themselves; particularly effective for bulimia and anorexia.

Chakra: Root and Solar Plexus.

Wearing blood agate or carrying a tiny blood agate egg is powerful in fertility problems where stress spoils lovemaking; it helps girls with late-onset puberty make the transition to womanhood.

Its power lies in the restoration of good health, employment and lasting love. It is helpful in keeping to fitness regimes or persisting with business ventures. As an additional boost for an all-or-nothing moment, combine blood agate with red jasper, but avoid overload. Blood agate overcomes a fear of spiders and discourages them in the home.

Candle colour: *Red.*
Fragrances: *Allspice, cinnamon, dragon's blood, ginger, hibiscus.*
Practical uses: *Restores passion in love and life.*
Magical significance: *Used by the Vikings in axe divination to find lost objects or hidden treasure; hold in closed hands until warm to know where and how to find what you need, whether lost or undiscovered.*
Divinatory meaning: *If you really want something, fight for it; if not, let it go.*
Zodiac: *Aries.*
Empowerment: *Life pulsates within me.*

RED TIGER'S EYE/OX EYE

Type: Oxide, quartz.

Colours: Banded gleaming reds.

Availability: Common.

Physical benefits: Seen as assisting anaemia, blood and blood cell disorders, eye infections and night vision, overall body strength and vitality, libido in both sexes, sexual dysfunction and potency in men, menstruation, psychosomatic illnesses, recovery after major surgery.

Emotional healing: Fills its wearer with enthusiasm and optimism if depressed; calms anger and irritability, especially in men.

Chakra: Sacral and Solar Plexus.

Red tiger's eye occurs when the golden-brown variety is exposed to heat, such as fire or lightning, but most on the commercial market is artificially heat-treated. This does not affect its metaphysical qualities.

All colours of tiger's eye are chatoyant, meaning it reflects iridescent light from its surface like a cat's eye. This effect is best when a stone is cut *en cabochon* (shaped and polished). Red tiger's eye makes fabulous jewellery for women fighting sexism or trying to succeed in a male-dominated firm without sacrificing femininity.

Associated with the strength and courage of the ox, it is a fierce defence worn round the neck against any kind of bullying. An antidote against anger, it can calm bullies.

Red tiger's eye will help in mediation and in releasing creative blocks. It is excellent if you are normally shy about being noticed and rewarded for your efforts.

Candle colour: *Red.*
Fragrances: *Allspice, cinnamon, dragon's blood, ginger, hibiscus.*
Practical uses: *In a situation where tempers are flaring or stress is reaching boiling point, place red tiger's eye tumblestones around the room. Wash them in very cold water afterwards.*
Magical significance: *For any urgent need light a red candle and surround it with eight small red tiger's eye crystals. Drip a tiny amount of melted wax on each stone; when the candle has burned through, carry the tiger's eyes in a small drawstring bag.*
Divinatory meaning: *Your efforts will be recognized as long as you do not let anyone else take credit for your ideas or input.*
Zodiac: *Aries and Taurus.*
Empowerment: *My efforts will bring results as long as I persevere.*

RUBELLITE

Type: Lithium-rich crystalline silicate.

Colours: Red, various shades from deep pink to rich red, resembling a ruby. The redder stones are more powerful.

Availability: Clear inclusion free rubellite is rare, but generally rubellite is relatively common.

Physical benefits: May help heart problems, physical energy, spleen and liver, anaemia, lung complaints, coughs and colds, muscle spasms and weakness.

Emotional healing: A powerful stone that strengthens and harmonizes the feminine within both sexes; makes women strong in emotional challenges. Men should not work with red tourmaline for prolonged periods of time.

Chakra: Root and Heart.

Candle colour: *Red or dark pink.*
Fragrances: *Chamomile, cherry blossom, gardenia, hyacinth, jasmine.*
Practical uses: *Bestows dignity, diplomacy and quiet authority if others are unreasonable or pulling rank.*
Magical significance: *Awakens passion and desire, especially in deeper red.*
Divinatory meaning: *There is an emotional challenge ahead; use your femininity to take a calm and gentle approach.*
Zodiac: *Libra and Scorpio.*
Empowerment: *Love will heal me and guide me.*

Rubellite (or Red Tourmaline) is effective in activating the Root chakra, without awakening aggression Circle at the tops of your thighs to restore vitality, libido, stamina and passion for life. You may experience tingling in your knees and feet as you circle your thighs. Keep the crystal moving until you feel a throbbing, rising warmth; do this weekly for vitality especially in winter. A shield against negativity: pass above your hair to clear your aura and make positive plans. Helps learning, and decisions that have long-term benefit.

ALMANDINE GARNET

Type: Silicate (iron aluminium silicate); often found combined with pyrope garnet.

Colours: Wine red to purple-red to red-black, brownish red. Precious garnet is deep red, transparent almandine.

Availability: Common unless with a star formation. Physical benefits: May help with pain, especially in childbirth, metabolism, wounds and cuts, menstruation, circulation, blood clots, haemophilia, gallstones, fertility, sexual potency and libido, DNA, immunity to colds and flu.

Emotional healing: Helps in bereavement

Chakra: Root and Heart.

Garnet is the name for a group of silicate minerals crystallized in a cubic system. The Crusaders wore almandine garnet rings to keep them safe.

Some rare almandine crystals from India or Idaho have asbestos inclusions that create a highly-prized, star-like effect when faceted; Almandine garnet prevents anger being directed inwards, which leads to stress-related conditions. Hold over your navel, your Sacral energy centre, and let the anger flow creatively or alternatively dissipate harmlessly outside your energy field.

Candle colour: *Red.*
Fragrances: *Angelica, bay, copal, rosemary.*
Practical uses: *Enduring passion for a person, hobby or cause.*
Magical significance: *Protection against emotional vampires, manipulators and evil spirits. Anyone engaged in spirit rescue should wear it.*
Divinatory meaning: *Look at who is draining your emotional energies*
Zodiac: *Capricorn and Aquarius.*
Empowerment: *I need not doubt my love will last.*

RED ZIRCON

Type: Silicate/nesosilicate, zircon.

Colours: Rich red, red-orange, red-violet and dark red.

Availability: Relatively common.

Physical benefits: Believed to help with infections and viruses; relieve pain, speeds healing of wounds and bruises; protect against MRS, C. Difficile, Norovirus and modern bugs that spread rapidly; ease insomnia, ear infections, liver, gall bladder and intestines.

Emotional healing: Brings peace after turmoil, sleep after wakefulness, renewed vitality after exhaustion and a sense of personal blessings after misfortune.

Chakra: Root and Heart.

Jacinth is referred to in the New Testament as one of the foundation stones of the heavenly Jerusalem. It was worn as protection against the Black Death in the 1300s and against the Great Plague of London in 1665. Red zircon is also called hyacinth after the flower created by Apollo when his love Hyakinthos was killed. Red zircon (also called Jacinth) is an anti-theft crystal. It was said to lose its sheen in the presence of plague, so be wary if your zircon becomes dull after spending time with someone, as they may be draining you.

Candle colour: *Red.*
Fragrances: *Carnation, cinnamon, hyacinth, saffron, sage.*
Practical uses: *Use for official correspondence, job or loan applications to ensure a favourable response.*
Magical significance: *Use as a love charm and to increase personal charisma; rub a cross shape over your zircon to deter jealous love rivals.*
Divinatory meaning: *If you really want something, now is the time to go all-out with power and passion.*
Zodiac: *Leo and Sagittarius.*
Empowerment: *I feel the surge of renewed enthusiasm, for life.*

RED AVENTURINE

Type: Microcrystalline quartz, sometimes containing inclusions of haematite to give a metallic, iridescent glint.

Colours: Red.

Availability: Common.

Physical benefits: May help reproductive system, fertility, speeds metabolism, lower cholestero, be helpful for side effects of radiotherapy, haemophilia, skin conditions especially eczema, fungal conditions, low blood pressure, pulse and irregular heartbeat, fibromyalgia, hernia.

Emotional healing: Restores good humour; increases libido if worn or placed beneath the mattress.

Chakra: Root and Solar Plexus.

Traditionally used against theft, fire, and lightning strikes. Protective against traffic accidents; place one in your car if you drive frequently.

Brings good luck when the odds are against you – hold a very small crystal, call out your need, then throw it as far as possible; the finder will be lucky too. A dish of red aventurines creates harmony between brothers and sisters. Wear if organizing a children's party, attending a family social event or meeting relatives who always find fault, to enable you to take everything in your stride.

Candle colour: *Red.*
Fragrances: *Allspice, cedar, copal, mint, saffron.*
Practical uses: *Good for weight problems*
Magical significance: *Brings money when carried in a small red bag with a sprinkling of spice such as ginger or cinnamon; for fertility substitute dried rosemary or dried rose petals.*
Divinatory meaning: *Your integrity and hard work will bring you success over a ruthless rival.*
Zodiac: *Aries.*
Empowerment: *As I wish so shall it be, as long as my heart is pure and my intention good.*

RUBY

Type: Corundum (aluminium oxide silicate).

Colours: Pinkish red, purple-red, deep rich to dark ruby red; the most valuable are deep red with a slight blue tinge called pigeon's blood ruby.

Availability: Common to relatively rare, depending on quality and colour.

Physical benefits: May help with infections, circulation, heart, energy, female fertility, male impotence; menstrual problems, early menopause, fibromyalgia, gynaecological operations, pregnancy – particularly for older women.

Emotional healing: Helps the sharing of loving energy despite past hurt; reduces fear of the paranormal and evil.

Chakra: Heart.

Candle colour: *Red.*
Fragrances: *Allspice, basil, carnation, cinnamon, dragon's blood, red rose.*
Practical uses: *Protects the home from fire and intruders; wear discreetly to stay safe at night.*
Workplace: *Increases profile and prosperity.*
Magical significance: *Guards against psychic and psychological attack (it is said to darken in the presence of a liar); wear during lovemaking to conceive and maintain/restore passion.*
Divinatory meaning: *Value friends and family even if they seem temporarily dull.*
Zodiac: *Cancer and Sagittarius.*
Empowerment: *My fears have no reality and I let them go.*

The ruby is one of the four precious gemstones (the others are diamond, emerald and sapphire), worn since ancient times to signify high status.

It is most commonly associated with love, especially faithful passionate commitment., and helps older women to value their beauty and life experience. Rubies bring prophetic dreams and banish nightmares; to dream of rubies is a sign of coming prosperity and good fortune.

Tumblestones at home for each family member will maintain loving links wherever they are.

COPPER DENDRITE

Type: Metal, dendrite, looks like copper leaf or made into different forms.

Colours: Golden-red burnished bronze.

Availability: Common.

Physical benefits: Thought to improve blood, circulation, exhaustion, toxicity, rheumatism, arthritis, stiffness and swellings of hands and feet, inflammation, weight loss, fertility, libido, particularly in women, metabolism, balance.

Emotional healing: Removes emotional burdens if worn on the hand you do not write with. Once a week, pass nine times over a green plant to clear energies.

Chakra: Heart

Copper jewellery has been worn since ancient times and is used in sacred offerings and to purify water. It was sacred to love goddesses, including the Greek Aphrodite and her Roman counterpart Venus (it is the metal of her planet).

Copper leaves are a good-luck charm, placed in a small green bag – the colour of Venus. Wrap them in cloth, one for health or money, two for love, three for a baby.

Add basil for money, rosemary for fertility and lavender or rose for love, tie with green ribbon in three knots. Protects against love rivals.

Candle colour: *Green.*

Fragrances: *Clary sage, eucalyptus, pine, vervain, vanilla.*

Practical uses: *Activates our instinctive radar and ability to find lost items or pets.*

Magical significance: *Copper tubing makes the ultimate magic wand as copper conducts energy to and from the spiritual world. Point outwards to call what you need and towards your body to energize you.*

Divinatory meaning: *Someone becomes friendlier, including you in a social event.*

Zodiac: *Taurus.*

Empowerment: *I am worth knowing.*

Tangerine Quartz

Type: Silicon dioxide, naturally occurring quartz permanently coated with haematite or iron.

Colours: Orange and the clear crystal can be seen within. Availability: From specialist mineral stores and online. Physical benefits: May assist assimilation of iron and minerals, healthy weight loss, reproductive problems, HIV and Aids, sexual dysfunction, recovery after an accident or trauma; abdomen, lower back, Seasonal Affective Disorder.

Emotional healing: Balancing for sex addiction, for those who love too much or who are afraid to make love.

Chakra: Sacral.

Tangerine quartz grows in enriched soil in lands as far apart as Brazil and Madagascar where it has been called the fruit-of-the-earth stone. However it is worn or used, tangerine quartz enriches life in the here-and-now, encouraging pleasure in what you have and who you are. Give tangerine quartz to anyone who is depressed, down on their luck, or who has been ill to become aware of possibilities and to contact friends and family again.
  A natural health-bringer, especially in winter.
  Exotic cat breeds thrive in the presence of this crystal.

Candle colour: *Orange.*
Fragrances: *Carnation, geranium, hibiscus, neroli, orange.*
Practical uses: *A stone of fertility, creativity and ingenuity. Wear if you are short of money to maximize your resources.*
Magical significance: *Encourages passion and fertility. Hold on your navel for five minutes to activate desire and confidence in your sexual charisma;*
Divinatory meaning: *Enjoy the present, adapt what you have and breathe new life into it.*
Zodiac: *Sagittarius.*
Empowerment: *I awaken desire for happiness.*

HONEY/AMBER CALCITE

Type: Calcium carbonate.

Colours: Pale to golden honey, amber.

Availability: Relatively common.

Physical benefits: Thought to help assist cell, skin and tissue regeneration, diabetes and all blood sugar fluctuations, fertility, bites and stings, back, spine, colon, digestion, intestines, liver, gall bladder, pancreas, spleen, nausea; infections when they first appear, bedwetting and stress incontinence, increased libido; and for encouraging healthy growth in children.

Emotional healing: A nurturing feel-good stone, especially for older women who have had emotional problems and lack self-esteem after the menopause; also for any woman after a hysterectomy who mourns the loss of her fertility and feels she is no longer sexually desirable.

Chakra: Solar Plexus.

Candle colour: *Natural beeswax.*

Fragrances: *Carnation, cloves, honey, marigold, peach.*

Practical uses: *Put honey calcite tumblestones on the table at family celebrations to bring happiness and stop rivalries flaring up; for harmony and a sense of blessings at mealtimes, whether eating alone or with others; helpful if a family member has an eating disorder, to prevent mealtimes becoming a battle.*

Magical significance: *The ultimate abundance-bringing crystal, especially if you can find a piece of honeycomb; surround it with golden-coloured crystals, flowers, fruit and jewellery, and regularly light beeswax candles to attract abundance or fertility.*

Divinatory meaning: *Do not worry about not having enough: things will manifest as most needed.*

Zodiac: *Sagittarius and Pisces.*

Empowerment: *I lack nothing.*

As well as ordinary honey calcite, a rare form of honeycomb calcite is found only in Utah. Created by the growth of long fibrous or tubular cells, it looks like petrified honey and is a natural beaty.

The honey colour means it is associated with the Virgin Mary and her mother Anne, the patroness of beekeepers. It is also linked with the Neolithic bee goddess tradition. Put a piece in the garden to help flowers and herbs flourish, and attract bees, butterflies and dragonflies.

Use honey calcite for networking, especially online; good for cyber love that thrives in the everyday world.

CITRINE

Type: Quartz, heated naturally in the earth.

Colours: Yellow and transparent, from pale to golden yellow, honey or almost brown; may contain rainbows and sparkles.

Availability: Relatively rare, but worth obtaining.

Physical benefits: Said to be good for relieving skin problems and allergies, especially those caused by food or chemical intolerances, liver problems and liver transplants, short-term memory loss, bedwetting particularly in young adults; fibromyalgia, nausea and vomiting; morning sickness.

Emotional healing: Effective against being a workaholic, stress leading to over-spending or excessive risk-taking, gambling addictions; neuroses of all kinds.

Chakra: Solar Plexus.

Natural citrine is said to contain solidified sunlight and never to absorb negativity and so never needs cleansing; wear as a shield against spite and jealousy, at the same time benefiting from its wealth- and luck-bringing powers. Natural citrine has all the powers and healing properties of heat-treated citrine but its energies are more powerful if less instant. Give as an angel or sphere to a newborn to bring intelligence, health, happiness, curiosity, money, confidence,, and above all healing wisdom. Carry to attract love and protect against those who would break your heart.

Candle colour: *Yellow.*
Fragrances: *Almond, lemon balm, orange.*
Practical uses: *A pyramid or geode attracts health and abundance to the home and spreads sunshine and happiness.*
Magical significance: *Natural citrine tumblestones where light catches them clear unfriendly ghosts; sprinkle citrine elixir weekly to prevent negative energies returning.*
Divinatory meaning: *A time to communicate your ideas and needs clearly.*
Zodiac: *Gemini.*
Empowerment: *I attract abundance into my life.*

Yellow Fluorite

Type: Halide/calcium fluoride.

Colours: Yellow.

Availability: One of the less common fluorites.

Physical benefits: May relieve problems with cholesterol, liver, bile, stomach adhesions, intestinal blockages or growths, stomach-stapling operations, cosmetic surgery, DNA, arthritis, rheumatism, spine, bones, teeth particularly wisdom teeth and gum health, shingles.

Emotional healing: For self-defeating behaviour and constantly comparing oneself unfavourably with others; reduces jealousy through insecurity and lack of self-love.

Chakra: Sacral and Solar Plexus.

Carry if you are naturally gentle and spiritual to direct intellect and effort into tangible achievements. If you find it hard to organize your thoughts or produce specifically defined results because your imagination takes off, use as an elixir or wear the crystal. Steers the fine path between attainable dreams and illusions; ideal for young people who are reluctant to begin a career from the bottom. Keep in the workplace or in organizing ventures where cooperation is needed
   A crystal to hold when you need to come up with a plausible excuse to avoid an event you are dreading.

Candle colour: *Yellow.*
Fragrances: *Chamomile, lavender, lemongrass, lemon verbena, sage.*
Practical uses: *Counteracts the tendency of caring people to give the coat off their back to every hard-luck story they come across.*
Magical significance: *Good for paranormal investigations or experiments to maintain objectivity without sacrificing intuition.*
Divinatory meaning: *You need to use logic and uncharacteristic toughness to resolve a problem.*
Zodiac: *Gemini*
Empowerment: *I can be strong and spiritual.*

LEMON QUARTZ

Type: Silicon dioxide/quartz; occurs naturally. Lemon colour caused by iron; also called oro verde.

Colours: Golden yellow-green, lemon.

Availability: Common.

Physical benefits: May relieve issues with nausea, bladder and kidneys, brain functioning, diabetes, lack of energy; for speeding recovery from an operation or prolonged illness, detoxify, increase metabolism and assist any weight-loss programme, clear colds that linger and infections of the skin.

Emotional healing: A a reminder of all the good things in life and blessings to counteract negativity.

Chakra: Solar Plexus.

Lemon quartz is faster-acting than citrine; wear for examinations or interviews. Use for making instant decisions, and for acquiring money fast in an emergency. Often worn by ghost investigators if the nature of a haunting is unknown or there is poltergeist activity.

One of the most effective crystals to wear to break the hold of someone who plays mind games, wear as earrings if the person uses flattering words to break down resistance. Reduces cravings, particularly for cigarettes and for food-related issues where binge and fasting create fluctuating weight; a prosperity-bringer.

Candle colour: *Lemon yellow.*
Fragrances: *Lemon, lemongrass, lime, neroli.*
Practical uses: *Brings good luck and a flow of fresh energies.*
Magical significance: *Said traditionally to have power against snake venom, worn as a pendant it repels spite; spiral a lemon or lemongrass incense stick over it weekly to clear of human venom.*
Divinatory meaning: *Stay detached from an argument between friends.*
Zodiac: *Gemini.*
Empowerment: *I will use my head as well as my heart.*

GOLD

Type: Native element/precious metal.

Colours: Metallic yellow and gleaming.

Availability: Common.

Physical benefits: Called a master healer because it is said to help almost every condition and will amplify the strength of any other crystals, metal or substance used; particularly arthritis, heart and spine, circulation, nervous system and digestion, tissue regrowth.

Emotional healing: Dispels negative thoughts, reduces excessive, harmful actions and reactions; even the smallest amount of gold provides the incentive to dig oneself out of an emotional or life-situation hole.

Chakra: Brow and Crown.

Candle colour: *Gold or yellow.*
Fragrances: *Benzoin, cinnamon, frankincense, orange, rosemary.*
Practical uses: *Gold rings bring fidelity to those in a relationship "as long as the sun lasts", and protection from rivals; if you are single, a gold ring endows the confidence to approach the person you want to be with and fight to win the right love.*
Magical significance: *Gold is the metal of the sun, especially at noon, the time of the sun's greatest power, and at midsummer. On Midsummer Day at noon, drop a thin gold ring or earring in sunlit water for success during the year ahead.*
Divinatory meaning: *Now is the time to apply for a television reality show, attend an audition or job interview, or submit a creative work; success is around you.*
Zodiac: *Leo*
Empowerment: *I am pure gold.*

Gold has been associated in many lands and ages with the deities. The Ancient Egyptians believed that the skin of their gods was made of gold, and so some Pharaohs, notably Tutankhamun, were given a gold deathmask.

Pure gold is yellow in colour but is often alloyed with other minerals, such as silver or copper, to make it harder. Pure 24-carat gold is quite soft. Very malleable, it can be beaten into the finest of layers, called leaf, then used for decorative and artistic proposes.

Gold helps to clear emotional and psychic blockages caused by negativity. Used during meditation with angel crystals such as seraphinite, opal aura or angelite, gold can help you to connect with the angelic realms, especially the Archangel Michael, whose special metal is gold.

GOLDEN/ YELLOW CALCITE

Type: Calcium carbonate.

Colours: From pale yellow through shades of yellow to gold.

Availability: Common.

Physical benefits: Seen as aiding the detoxification of all digestive organs.

Emotional healing: Self-esteem that has been damaged by abuse, coldness or neglect in childhood or later in life by a destructive or controlling relationship; assists body-image issues.

Chakra: Solar Plexus and Sacral.

Use for healing pets or for soothing rescued or lost animals; add the natural crystal to pet water for a few hours; also helps pets who are jealous of a new family member to minimize aggression. Set tumbled stone in healing or home empowerment/protection layouts to spread the energy through the grid and into the patient or the home.The more golden the stone, the more powerful its properties; a golden calcite sphere expands the boundaries of what is possible through our own efforts rather than luck. An excellent crystal if you are a mature student or want to retrain.

Candle colour: *Gold.*
Fragrances: *Anise, copal, frankincense, sandalwood, sage.*
Practical uses: *Melts resentment and estrangement and, if worn, attracts friendships and social opportunities.*
Magical significance: *Write down the names of anyone spiteful, fold the list as small as possible and tie it with three knots with a piece of yellow calcite in a yellow scarf. Keep in a drawer.*
Divinatory meaning: *A routine social event will be better than expected. Accept the invitation.*
Zodiac: *Sagittarius and Pisces*
Empowerment: *I will make today golden.*

GOLDEN BERYL

Type: Beryl, ring silicate, also known as heliodor especially in its yellow-green variety.

Colours: Canary yellow to golden yellow.

Availability: Common.

Physical benefits: May help with liver, stomach, spleen, pancreas, small intestine, gallstones, glands, nausea and vomiting, diarrhoea and chronic constipation, preserve youthfulness, heart, for concussion and skull damage, Seasonal Affective Disorder, exhaustion.

Emotional healing: The ultimate confidence and wellbeing gem, often called the sunshine stone.

Chakra: Solar Plexus.

Protects against the psychological and emotional manipulation of others and from unfriendly ghosts, and general dark energies. A dish of tumblestones where sunlight will shine on them disperses spookiness and attracts angelic energies; good for couples whose relationship has lost its sparkle. Wear if you are impatient with others to develop empathy; for healers, medical personnel, call-centre staff, therapists, care workers and parents to hold in natural form towards the end of a long day to keep smiling. A good naming-day or christening gift for a child as a good-fairy gem.

Candle colour: *Bright yellow.*
Fragrances: *Chamomile, copal, marigold, sage, sunflower.*
Practical uses: *Increases the capacity to recall new information; good for study, especially for reluctant students.*
Magical significance: *Enables you to discover secrets about people's intentions. Close your eyes, hold between your hands, ask what you need to know and the names and information will come to you.*
Divinatory meaning: *Anything is possible right now with determination and effort.*
Zodiac: *Sagittarius.*
Empowerment: *I am motivated to succeed in any challenge.*

TIGER'S EYE

Type: Oxide, quartz.

Colours: Brown and gold striped; gleaming and chatoyant, reflecting light in wavy bands.

Availability: Common.

Physical benefits: May help to ease stomach and gallbladder problems, ulcers, sprains, rheumatism; increase energy levels and strength, restore balance to the body.

Emotional healing: Reduces cravings for the wrong kind of food, and binges on food, cigarettes, prescription drugs or alcohol; reduces anxiety caused by feelings of isolation or inadequacy; increases willpower and emotional stability to make health-improving regimes more likely to succeed.

Chakra: Root and Solar Plexus.

Candle colour: *Gold.*
Fragrances: *Bay, carnation, copal, geranium, saffron, spearmint.*
Practical uses: *Attracts the steady inflow of money. Place a tiger's eye in a pot with a lid and add a coin every day. When full, spend the money on something fun or give to charity and start again.*
Magical significance: *A traditional protection against the evil eye; carry or wear a tiger's eye to ward off jealousy, whether from a partner's ex, sibling rivalry or envious colleagues.*
Divinatory meaning: *Money-making ventures and new projects will succeed better than anticipated if you persist and keep focused when you hit an obstacle.*
Zodiac: *Leo*
Empowerment: *I am filled with golden light and can reach out in the confidence that I will succeed.*

Associated with the tiger, the king of beasts in Eastern mythology. Roman soldiers carried tiger's eye to be brave in battle. To the Ancient Egyptians, tiger's eye offered the protection of both Ra, the sun god and Geb, the god of the growing land.

The eye formation protects by reflecting back any malice from others. To know whether a person or offer is reliable, hold a tiger's eye and trust your feelings. Traditionally it is said by the end of the day, any deception will be revealed or known.

If you seek to test a creative talent in public or to sell your gifts in the market place, tiger's eye will enable you to overcome a fear of failure and help you to shine. It also stops a pet trying to dominate the household or other animals.

BROWN JASPER

Type: Silicate, microcrystalline quartz, often with mineral or organic inclusions.

Colours: Varying shades of yellow to golden to reddish brown; some brown jaspers with particular pattern formations are given names such as "picture jasper".

Availability: Common.

Physical benefits: Seen to aid the bowels, anus, prostate, constant constipation, gastro-enteritis, IBS, coeliac disease, Crohn's disease, wheat and dairy allergies, feet, ankles, knees, joints, muscles, ligaments, fungus infections, warts, moles, verrucas, blisters, abscesses, rodent ulcers, genitals in both sexes, loss of libido, dry skin, kidney stones and kidney disease, tetanus, varicose veins.

Emotional healing: Reduces insecurity in those who are worried about losing their money, home or job, or who are filled with guilt about past failings and inadequacies; breaks the self-defeating cycle and brings contentment.

Chakra: Root.

In Ancient Egypt, brown jasper was called Egyptian marble and used for amulets, ritual vessels and jewellery. It was carved into arrow-heads in North America and prized as a luck bringer.

  Use brown jasper as a charm for all property matters and for success in meetings about finances. Wear it when trying to quit smoking and to stop a panic attack. It makes an excellent worry stone if you are pressurized at work. Gives stamina to old or sick animals and restores natural instincts to a pet living in the city.

Candle colour: *Brown.*
Fragrances: *Anise, cinnamon, cloves, pine, thyme.*
Practical uses: *Good for bringing yourself down to earth if you are panicking or angry; wear brown jasper jewellery, touch it and press down hard with your feet, letting all the tension, fury or fear sink down so you relax.*
Magical significance: *Among Native North Americans brown was prized along with green jasper as a rain-bringer and was rubbed to call the rains; shake your jasper between cupped hands or on the surface of a drum, reciting your need faster and faster and shaking or rattling till you end with a final call and rattle.*
Divinatory meaning: *Stay calm and be realistic about obstacles ahead; things will work out well, if slower than expected.*
Zodiac: *Capricorn.*
Empowerment: *I have no need to panic.*

53

PETRIFIED/FOSSILIZED WOOD

Type: Wood that comes from fossilized trees in which the wood is replaced over many millions of years by a mineral, usually quartz or agate, that assumes the shape of the original tree.

Colours: Usually brown or grey-brown, grey, black, red, pink/orange, fawn, may be banded and include white (colour varies according to the impurities).

Availability: Common.

Physical benefits: Claimed to relieve back and hip pain, strengthens bones and skeletal alignment; help illness that is difficult to diagnose or treat, progressive or periodically recurring illnesses, mobility problems and those linked with the ageing process; be beneficial for bad backs, allergies, bone dislocation and broken limbs and hay fever.

Emotional healing: Heals relationships that cannot be put right on the earth plane because the person who hurt you has died; helps to recall fond memories of deceased relations who found it hard to express emotions.

Chakra: Root and Sacral.

Petrified wood offers insight to access past lives through regression. A stone of transformation, to let go of what no longer works in our lives while preserving what is still of value.

During meditation or healing work, petrified wood provides protection from negative energies and afterwards grounds your energies; encourages a child to take an interest in their family origins. The crystal is beneficial to skin and hair as an elixir.

Candle colour: *Brown.*
Fragrances: *Basil, cedar, cypress, juniper, moss, vetivert.*
Practical uses: *Petrified wood is helpful for those living in older buildings to keep the structure sound; put pieces in the attic near rafters and in basements and in any walls or fireplaces you renovate.*
Magical significance: *Brings positive contact with beloved deceased relations through dreams and unmistakable signs of their presence; connects you with family ancestors who act as your spirit guardians.*
Divinatory meaning: *Time to let go of a friendship or activity that no longer brings pleasure and is starting to make you feel trapped.*
Zodiac: *Virgo*
Empowerment: *I welcome the wisdom that comes with age.*

PUMICE STONE

Type: Volcanic rock containing many bubbles.

Colours: Pale coloured, fawn to light grey or tan, occasionally black if it contains a lot of iron and magnesium.

Availability: Common.

Physical benefits: May ease pain, especially menstrual, painful muscles, locked joints, skin complaints and allergies, abrasions and bruises; traditionally said to ease labour pain; also useful for scars and scar tissue, lesions, ulcers; help any degenerative condition, particularly of the brain.

Emotional healing: Enables repressed anger to flow away; good for those who have accumulated heavy emotional luggage over years to gradually put them down.

Chakra: Solar Plexus.

Some of the lava that spews out of the volcanoes has bubbles of gas trapped in it. This form of lava is called pumice. Because of its dynamic creation, pumice is a stone of power; people who use it on their feet are filling their Root energy centre with stamina and earth power as a bonus. Massage the soles of your feet with pumice any time you know people or situations during the day ahead may unsettle you; this will fill you with courage and confidence. Because of the rough texture of pumice and its ability to float on water, it became associated with cleansing and beautifying.

Candle colour: *Grey.*
Fragrances: *Almond, bergamot, sweetgrass.*
Practical uses: *Keep a small pile in a jar near a source of heat at home so that absent family and friends recall the warmth and keep in touch; also to draw good fortune and protect against fire and flood.*
Magical significance: *The holes in pumice can be used for whispering wishes and then floated away in running water.*
Divinatory meaning: *Listen to your head and heart.*
Zodiac: *Aries.*
Empowerment: *I attract good luck and happiness.*

AMMONITE/SNAKE/ SERPENT STONES

Type: Fossilized sea creatures that first appeared about 435 million years ago and inhabited the sea in great numbers, living in the spiral shell now found as the ammonite fossil; the incredibly rare iridescent ammolite gem is formed from mineralized ammonites.

Colours: Brown, grey or fawn.

Availability: Relatively common.

Physical benefits: Can alleviate problems with genetically transmitted diseases, relieve chronic cramps and erectile dysfunction. Also a good-luck charm for pregnancy, believed to be beneficial for health in the over-eighties and in childbirth as a pain reliever.

Emotional healing: Protective against repeating old mistakes and from getting stuck in outmoded family roles; soothing near the cradle for babies after birth trauma such as prolonged or emergency deliveries and Caesareans.

Chakra: Root.

Beloved by the Ancient Egyptians and Ancient Greeks and named after the Egyptian creator god Amun, ammonite was considered by the Romans to hold the power of prophecy. A myth from Whitby, northeast England, identifies ammonites as snakes killed in AD 657 by St Hilda, who turned all the snakes into stone on the land where she wanted to found her abbey; a similar legend concerns St Keyna at Keynsham, near Bristol.

Holding an ammonite assists recall of the Akashic records, the spiritual collective store of wisdom past, present and future.

Candle colour: *Brown or grey.*
Fragrances: *Cypress, lilac, patchouli, sweetgrass, vervain, vetivert.*
Practical uses: *Ammonite brings lasting health, wealth and happiness.*
Magical significance: *Place an ammonite next to your bed to bring dreams of past worlds, especially legendary lost sea lands such as Atlantis, Arthurian Lyonesse and Lemuria, and for prophetic dreams.*
Divinatory meaning: *Do not repeat past mistakes, but use your experience to maximize a new opportunity.*
Zodiac: *Cancer*
Empowerment: *I do not fear ageing but welcome wisdom that comes from experience.*

STROMATOLITE

Type: Micro fossils.

Colours: Often golden brown and deep brown but they can include grey, tan and sandy; beautiful when polished.

Availability: Rare but obtainable online and in some specialist mineral stores.

Physical benefits: Viewed as assisting with memory, eye problems, throat, teeth, bones, headaches and nervous system; helping with maintaining health in people in their eighties onwards, building resistance to debilitating diseases, the release of harmonious flow of bodily fluids.

Emotional healing: Brings profound healing from deep within the earth, alleviating even overwhelming stress and triggering positive energies for an emotional turnaround.

Chakra: Crown and Brow.

Stromatolites are actually fossils and are among the earliest forms of life.

As with all fossils, stromatolite is a useful aid in past-life recall, shamanic journeying and regression, as well as for contemplative meditation. Run your index finger repetitively and slowly over a highly patterned large stromatolite palm or worry stone until you achieve an almost trance-like state.

A stromatolite in the home encourages love of family traditions and heritage, and can help adopted children to discover and value their birth-roots without rejecting their adoptive family; good for merging family cultural and religious values with those of the wider community or if you find that your loyalties are divided.

Candle colour: *Any earth colour.*

Fragrances: *Geranium, lilac, moss, patchouli, vervain.*

Practical uses: *Hold stromatolite to your forehead to ground you or if people are questioning and correcting you and you feel insecure. Visualize energy flowing from the earth, materializing as roots that grow into the ground beneath your feet as certainty.*

Magical significance: *Buy a polished stromatolite sphere or egg; sit outdoors on the ground when sun or moonlight shines on the surface. Patterns on the surface will form images and suggest words in your mind to convey the wisdom of Mother Earth.*

Divinatory meaning: *Advice from an older person who seemed out of touch will help to resolve a hidden worry.*

Zodiac: *Capricorn.*

Empowerment: *My roots are deep and draw on ancient wisdom.*

SIDERITE

Type: Iron carbonate.

Colours: Brown, pale yellow, brownish yellow, greenish brown, reddish brown, sometimes iridescent or pearly. Availability: Relatively common, although good collectible specimens are rare.

Physical benefits: Seen as useful for strength and vitality' beneficial for skeletal system, chronic digestive and bowel disorders caused or made worse by food allergies, dizziness that does not have a specific physical cause, poor balance.

Emotional healing: Gives the courage to speak out against and act independently of controlling or super-critical relatives who try to rule adult life.

Chakra: Root.

At times of weakness, hold siderite and allow its energies to recharge yourself. It is particularly potent if you are naturally shy. If you feel constantly unenthusiastic, it can trigger your inner passions.
  Overuse of this crystal may cause a power struggle within an unsteady relationship as siderite has powerfully assertive energies. To counterbalance this, add copper or rose quartz for gentler feelings. Keep near stairs if you live with people who have a tendency to trip. Use to inspire loyalty. Keep in your car if you have an interfering passenger and to keep focused.

Candle colour: *Yellow or bronze.*
Fragrances: *Allspice, basil, dragon's blood, galangal, tarragon.*
Practical uses: *A comforting stone to display at home when relatives who disrupt your life visit. If you are alone at night, siderite calms fears.*
Magical significance: *An amulet against bad luck, the carelessness of others, breakages, breakdown of vehicles or equipment and accidents.*
Divinatory meaning: *Be careful not to be swept away by someone else's infatuation.*
Zodiac: *Aries.*
Empowerment: *I will not fail.*

CERUSITE

Type: Lead carbonate, white lead ore, beautiful twinned crystals and clusters or star shapes.

Colours: Brown, clear, misty white, sparkling.

Availability: Obtainable from specialist mineral stores and online. Occasionally found in jewellery.

Physical benefits: Believed to help balance the brain's hemispheres; assist with relief Alzheimer's, senile dementia, Parkinson's disease, prostate problems, bones, arthritis and rheumatism, any illness with an unpredictable pattern.

Emotional healing: Helps with addictions, fears of ageing, chronic depression or acute pessimism; sleep disorders.

Chakra: Root and Crown

Cerusite is good for practical matters, property and financial stability, and is associated with good luck in speculation. A crystal of increasing self-confidence through developing competence. Cerusite will help anyone involved in financial institutions, museums, teachers of history, religion and all who collect and communicate myths. Keep a small piece, well wrapped, with amazonite and green aventurine in a small bag with lottery numbers or any form of speculation where there is a random element. **WARNING:** It is toxic. Do not use in elixirs, ingest or keep near children or pets.

Candle colour: *Brown.*
Fragrances: *Anise, fern, mimosa, myrrh, patchouli.*
Practical uses: *Keep in the home or workplace in the weeks before any planned change to ease the transition.*
Magical significance: *Connects us with our spiritual side and the more evolved parts of the mind. This increases our intuitive and psychic powers; keep a cluster on the central table during collective spiritual activities.*
Divinatory meaning: *A certainty suddenly becomes less so.*
Zodiac: *Capricorn.*
Empowerment: *I can adapt to any changes demanded of me.*

DINOSAUR BONE

Type: Agatized dinosaur bone is fossilized bone from dinosaurs in which the cellular structure has been replaced with quartz, leaving the bone structure intact.

Colours: Brown, grey, white or black for natural; agatized as brown to black with splashes of red, blue and bright yellow; occasionally yellow-gold and red.

Availability: Becoming rarer as collection is restricted. Physical benefits: Said to be good for bone strength and fracture healing, bone marrow, DNA and all hereditary conditions, relief of chronic pain, lifelong illnesses.

Emotional healing: Soothes grief after the death of a long-term mate, a child or the breakdown of a relationship.

Chakra: Root.

Even the smallest piece of fossilized bone carries millions of years of the world's history within it; totally natural relics are even more magical than their more polished cousins. Hold when you are tired or others are taking your power away; draw strength from accumulated ancient Earth power, one of the most powerful and yet soothing energizers; bury a small natural dinosaur bone near the doorstep of a newly built house or in any wall, fireplace, new conservatory, extension or conversion. This will bring good fortune to the home and protect against teething problems.

Candle colour: *Grey.*
Fragrances: *Cypress, lavender, musk, sage*
Practical uses: *Good if you have older relatives living with you to help them feel part of the family.*
Magical significance: *Connects the wearer with the wisdom of many ages, bringing spontaneous recall of past lives and worlds.*
Divinatory meaning: *Do not make the same mistake you have done before when dealing with a manipulative person; stand strong.*
Zodiac: *Capricorn*
Empowerment: *The past holds the key to the future.*

ASTROPHYLLITE

Type: Titanium mineral, associated with feldspar, mica and titanite.

Colours: Golden yellow, red-brown, greenish brown or golden brown, with a metallic or pearly sheen.

Availability: Found in specialist crystal stores and online.

Physical benefits: Thought to help with cholesterol, reproductive organs, fertility, hormones, PMS, menopause, healthy cell regrowth, sensitivity to noise, light, chemical irritants or food.

Emotional healing: If you have been responsible for others from childhood, astrophyllite releases you from the feeling of needing to make others happy to follow your own path and desires.

Chakra: Crown

Astrophyllite has become associated with astrology and star wisdom. It eases the transition from one life stage to another. Holding by candle or moonlight reveals light at the end of the tunnel and may attract an unexpected new opportunity or a lifeline soon afterwards. Meditating will reveal your destiny and you will coincidentally meet the right people and chances in the weeks you work with the crystal to lead you on the unfolding path to realizing dreams alsoto visiting places again apparently coincidentally where you need to be to fulfil this blueprint.

Candle colour: *Gold or silver.*
Fragrances: *Acacia, almond, anise, copal.*
Practical uses: *Stroke when you feel anxious or irritable. It acts as an meditation tool and relaxant.*
Magical significance: *A crystal for astral travel, connects with UFO energies.*
Divinatory meaning: *You will get unexpected proof that your intuitions were accurate.*
Zodiac: *Cancer, Scorpio, and Capricorn.*
Empowerment: *I walk the path towards my true life's purpose.*

LAVA

Type: Volcanic rock.

Colours: Brown, grey or blackish, also blue.

Availability: Common.

Physical benefits: It is believed that pointed, pock-marked lava can draw out pain and illness; move the crystal down the body, flicking it away regularly during treatment towards the flame of a red candle to symbolically cleanse the lava; may also relieve chronic skin conditions.

Emotional healing: Made from solidified volcanic material, it increases vitality in those sunk into lethargy; good for the long-term unemployed or dispossessed to make effort in the face of discouragement.

Chakra: Solar Plexus.

Lava is sacred to Pele, the Hawaiian goddess of volcanoes, fire and magic. Sometimes smooth, rounded lava is regarded as female and is combined with the pointed pocked male lava in sex or fertility rituals or carried by a couple who want a baby. Wrap a piece of female lava in some greenery, tie it in with twine in three knots and set it on the earth facing west; ask that any misfortune may be taken away. Wear to shine in any situation and to attract passionate love; also good for earthing and containing irritability in anyone with a bad temper or who deliberately creates dramas.

Candle colour: *Red.*
Fragrances: *Allspice, copal, frankincense, saffron.*
Practical uses: *In the home or car it disarms troublemakers; protective also against fires, accidents and burglary.*
Workplace: *Have a small display of pointed and rounded lava. hold pointed lava outwards to guard against bad-tempered employers and colleagues; touch rounded lava to activate your energies.*
Magical significance: *Lava is very lucky because it involves the fusion of the four ancient magical elements.*
Divinatory meaning: *Wait until feelings have cooled before tackling an emotive issue.*
Zodiac: *Aries and Scorpio.*
Empowerment: *I value nature's gifts.*

Leopardskin Jasper

Type: Silicate, microcrystalline quartz, sister to rhyolite.

Colours: Tan, yellow, pink, red or beige with spots and bands of darker colour, sometimes glassy inclusions.

Availability: Common.

Physical benefits: May improve glands, hormones, bites and stings, nervous system affecting coordination, eczema, rashes and skin allergies, viruses and infections, urinary tract, lower digestive organs, reproductive system, hair parasites.

Emotional healing: Attracts the right energies into your life to move beyond past traumas and scars caused by being forced into conformity by severe discipline in early life.

Chakra: Root.

Works slowly so needs to be used or worn for long periods, next to the skin, to benefit fully from its supportive energies. It can be particularly beneficial to wear as beads around your wrist or neck for a few months to re-harmonize your internal mechanisms whilst on the outside you will repel situations that are not good. At the same time you will be guided to new opportunities and to view existing situations in new ways; you may find your soul mate was close by. It is a powerful animal healer for adult pets, but too powerful for small or young animals or children.

Candle colour: *Brown.*
Fragrances: *Chrysanthemum, fennel, lavender, lime.*
Practical uses: *Brings into our lives what we really need, restores sharpness and psychological hunting instincts.*
Magical significance: *Use to connect with your power animal and understand its purpose in your life; use with guided fantasy or drum music to travel astrally on the back of a magical animal to mystical realms.*
Divinatory meaning: *It is cold outside but you have waited enough.*
Zodiac: *Gemini and Scorpio*
Empowerment: *I will not question what life brings.*

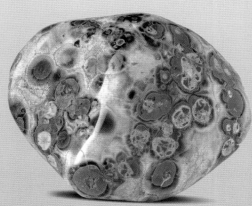

SUNSTONE

Type: Oligioclase feldspar.

Colours: Golden orange, red, red-brown, brown-orange and green with a sparkly iridescent sheen.

Availability: Clean red examples are very rare. Others are more common.

Physical benefits: May aid all lower-body ailments including the reproductive organs, digestion, stomach ulcers, prostate, feet, legs, Seasonal Affective Disorder, body odour.

Emotional healing: Excellent for easing phobias about the dark, enclosed places; also for any phobia sufferers, to become less fearful of the presence of their trigger.

Chakra: Root and Solar Plexus.

Candle colour: *Red.*
fragrances: *Benzoin, copal, cyphi, frankincense, honey.*
Practical uses: *Wear to feel alive and enthusiastic; also when starting a new exercise regime to give you the impetus to persevere.*
Magical significance: *Carry with moonstone to integrate god and goddess powers, animus and anima, assertive and outward success and inner harmony within your life.*
Divinatory meaning: *Enjoy the present without worrying if the good times will last.*
Zodiac: *Leo.*
Empowerment: *I am whole and happy.*

Sunstone is formed within lava and, once it is released on to the Earth's surface, weathering of the lava reveals the crystals hidden within. It therefore attracts unexpected prosperity by uncovering your talents.
   Attracts fame and good luck in competitions. Wear to lead you to the resources to travel and for happy holidays or relocation to the sun. It also protects you against those who drain your energies and finances and makes you tougher if people exploit you. An excellent crystal if you are dependent on others emotionally or have suffered sudden loss of a partner.

CLEAR CALCITE

Type: Calcium carbonate.

Colours: Clear, colourless.

Availability: Common.

Physical benefits: Labelled as an all-healer, it is said to cleanse organs connected with elimination and prevents calcification in bones; believed to be especially good as an elixir for intestines, skin, warts and ulcers and for detoxification; thought to assist healthy growth in children and growth disorders, improve eyesight, weight loss.

Emotional healing: Helpful for obsessive compulsive disorder, Tourette's syndrome, tics or any destructive or self-destructive behaviour.

Chakra: Crown.

Calcite is one of the world's most common and yet most diverse minerals: there are over three hundred calcite crystal forms recorded. Colourless or white is the purest form. In its most water-like transparent form, clear calcite is doubly refractive and called optical calcite or Iceland spar.

Colourless calcite is the best of the calcites for absent healing. A natural calcite or a cluster, sometimes attached to other minerals such as haematite or fluorite, is an excellent focus for transmitting light and healing from angels or healing guides via your fingers: hold the clear calcite and picture the person, animal or place to whom or which you are sending the healing.

A crystal for speaking the truth but with tact and compassion, especially if you are breaking bad news.

Candle colour: *White.*
Fragrances: *Almond, jasmine, mimosa, peach, white rose.*
Practical uses: *Helps you to find lost objects or papers; shine bright light on the surface and you will get a picture in your mind of where you left/lost the item.*
Magical significance: *A space clearer. Keep a small bowl of colourless calcite in the centre of any room where you meditate, practice therapies or magic, or where you sense negative paranormal activity; useful when moving into a home where the previous owner suffered divorce, illness or misfortune or the house has been empty. Wash crystals weekly under running water.*
Divinatory meaning: *A new beginning you seek may be taking longer than anticipated, but it will happen.*
Zodiac: *Aquarius.*
Empowerment: *I clear all clutter from my life.*

Snow/Milky Quartz

Type: Silicon dioxide, opaque quartz.

Colours: Polar white right through. Microscopic gas or water bubbles trapped in it cause the whiteness.

Availability: Common.

Physical benefits: Seen as good for bones, dislocation, bone marrow, breasts, teeth, absorption of calcium, lactation, infant feeding, blood disorders, fevers, menopausal symptoms, early-onset menopause, hysterectomy.

Emotional healing: After a family breach send snow-quartz carving or jewellery with a bridge-building note; in worst cases, circle a photo of the estranged person for a week with snow quartz before contact.

Chakra: Brow.

Candle colour: *White.*
Fragrances: *Almond, anise, magnolia, mimosa, neroli.*
Practical uses: *Against winter hazards. Keep in a car for winter starting or driving in snow; in hot climates dip it in cold water for cooling.*
Magical significance: *Set three snow quartz in a bowl of ice; let it melt, stirring, to soften coldness in a love affair or get luck flowing. Tip the melted ice into water and crystals into a small bag.*
Divinatory meaning: *Move forward with caution.*
Zodiac: *Capricorn.*
Empowerment: *Winter must come so spring will follow.*

Snow quartz is the crystal of the snow moon, the January or February full moon that American Indians called Gnawing on Bones Moon. In Scandinavia it heralds deep snow. It is said Mother Holle or Hulda waved her icicle wand that the land might sleep and grow strong, and snow quartz fell from it. Often called the female or yin version of clear quartz, with slower but more lasting energies, it is essential in a frantic environment. A snow quartz sphere slows everything and everyone down to avoid accidents, and improves productivity.

SNAKESKIN AGATE

Type: Chalcedony, crypto-crystalline quartz.

Colours: White or cream with a wrinkled or cracked surface resembling snakeskin; also found in green.

Availability: One of the less common agates.
Physical benefits: Thought to assist skin disorders, dry skin, eczema, skin parasites, warts, verruccas, melanomas, bites or stings, hearing problems, intestines, stomach disorders, weight loss, cosmetic surgery, liposuction, breast reduction, reconstructive surgery; regrowth of cells and muscles.

Emotional healing: Protective against false friends and bad influences for those who are innocents, so easily led astray and hurt again and again by betrayal or trickery.

Chakra: Root and Brow.

White snakeskin agate is sacred to the wise power serpent in the Native North American tradition.
  Like other swirling agate dream stones, it aids meditation and relaxation. Follow the patterns with your eye, let your mind go blank. Good for stamina, and should be worn by all doing heavy physical work, especially in the construction industry, as it protects against accidents. Take it on country trips to connect with nature; helps awaken teenagers who find it hard to leave technology.

Candle colour: *Cream.*
Fragrances: *Anise, basil, cloves, tarragon, sage.*
Practical uses: *Good for leaving a place where you have been unhappy or a relationship going nowhere, and for quitting smoking.*
Magical significance: *Said to make you less visible; hold agate and picture your energy field shrinking.*
Divinatory meaning: *Time to shed old burdens and plan new strategies: things are changing for the better.*
Zodiac: *Scorpio.*
Empowerment: *I can travel light.*

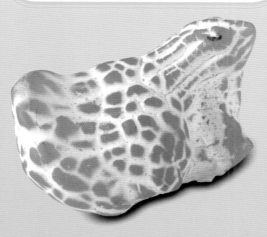

WHITE DOLOMITE

Type: Calcium magnesium carbonate.

Colours: Milky white, colourless, reddish white, brownish white, yellowish white, grey, pink, beige with pink hue, Availability: Relatively common.

Physical benefits: Viewed as being beneficial for bones, teeth, nails, skin, muscles; said to relieve PMS and menopausal symptoms, female reproductive problems, genito-urinary system in both sexes, asthma and emphysema, kidney stones, blood cells, oxygenation of lungs, colds, coughs, chills, adrenal glands, heart, circulation, cramps, insomnia.

Emotional healing: Prevents energy from draining away on useless causes or emotionally demanding people; brings comfort when all hope is lost, and friends and loved ones are far away or have deserted you.

Chakra: Heart.

Candle colour: *White.*
Fragrances: *Almond blossom, apple blossom, hyacinth, lilac, white roses.*
Practical uses: *The charitable crystal, dolomite attracts backing for voluntary initiatives and fund-raising activities; supportive for all who care for those with disabilities or serious illnesses and children with severe behavioural difficulties.*
Magical significance: *A stone of small miracles, when logical means have failed; hold your dolomite on your navel and focus on the attainment; repeat morning and evening, and each time add to the sensation of experiencing the fulfilment.*
Divinatory meaning: *Everything happens for a reason so look at a delay as a chance to reassess and maybe adjust your direction.*
Zodiac: *Taurus.*
Empowerment: *I do not fear being alone.*

Discovered in the 1790s in the Swiss Alps by an explorer called Dolomieu, the crystal is said to be stored treasure belonging to gnomes who have forgotten to collect it. For this reason dolomite in the home will attract enough for your needs – and a bit more.

An anti-jealousy stone, dolomite soothes the insecure so that they can enjoy a relationship without fearing betrayal or testing their partner's loyalty; also makes a possessive partner or parent relax.

Dolomite is a stone for those suffering from poor health, as it builds up stamina and resistance to illness. It soothes over-anxious children and animals, and is a calming influence in the nursery.

MILKY OPAL

Type: Hydrated silicon dioxide, generally common opal, though the name is sometimes applied to milky-white opalescent precious opal or opals with light backgrounds.

Colours: Milky white to light grey and translucent (cloudy).

Availability: Common.

Physical benefits: Said to assist with fertility and pregnancy, to act as an aid to labour and to soothe mother and child in the post-natal phase; help feeding difficulties, particularly mastitis; all breast problems in women of any age, cell regeneration, mucous membranes, coughs, lung congestion, skin, fluid imbalances and hormones, Alzheimer's disease and dementia, especially in women.

Emotional healing: For overcoming fears of childbirth that prevent a woman from trying for a baby; overwhelming fears during pregnancy and early months of a baby's life about infant mortality or disability, especially if there were problems with an earlier pregnancy.

Chakra: Sacral and Heart.

Milk opals were known as the milk drops of the mother goddess in a number of cultures. They are a popular gift for a new mother after the birth of a child.

Milky opal eases a child into school or daycare; surround a photograph of the child with small milky opals while they are away to send loving and secure vibes to the child. Bury a tiny milky opal beneath a willow, the mother tree or any fruit tree at full moon to conceive a child.

Candle colour: *Cream.*
Fragrances: *Apple blossom, cherry blossom, lemon balm, lemon verbena, neroli.*
Practical uses: *Milky opal creates a warm, safe environment if you care for foster children, or your own or a partner's children are behaving badly to test your affection.*
Magical significance: *Milky opals were once considered to have the power to confer invisibility in danger. Today they can be used to maintain a low profile. Breathe gently on your opal and picture its milkiness enclosing you in a soft cloud until the difficult situation has passed.*
Divinatory meaning: *A time for caring for a vulnerable person who is too proud to ask for help but who is struggling.*
Zodiac: *Cancer.*
Empowerment: *I can meet my own needs.*

SATIN SPAR

Type: Gypsum, the fibrous version; satin spar in its polished form sometimes mistaken for its very close sister selenite, another form of gypsum.

Colours: White and always glowing translucent/opalescent with bands of moving white light that resemble satin; also less commonly brown, orange, pink, yellow, green.

Availability: Common.

Physical benefits: Considered to help regularize women's hormones and menstrual cycles, to ease migraines and visual disturbances caused by PMS; may help scar tissue, speedy recovery after operations, especially gynaecological ones and Caesareans, bones, particularly osteoporosis, skin health.

Emotional healing: A dual-purpose crystal to calm when life gets too stressed and hectic, and energize when you are feeling lethargic or uninspired; soothing for hyperactive adults and children.

Chakra: Sacral.

In Ancient Greece satin spar was believed to have been part of the moon goddess's robe, discarded after she danced at full moon. In wand form, programme other crystals with it for specific healing purposes by moving clockwise over them, then anti-clockwise after use to clear and again clockwise to reprogramme. It will also cleanse and empower any spiritual artefacts. For gentle healing set satin spar on all seven chakra energy centres.

Candle colour: *Silver.*
Fragrances: *Jasmine, lemon, mimosa, myrrh, poppy.*
Practical uses: *A good-luck crystal particularly for love, money, travel and fertility; recharge by leaving it in full moonlight.*
Magical significance: *Take satin spar into full or nearly full moonlight; do nothing, say nothing, but absorb the lunar energies and let peace flow through you.*
Divinatory meaning: *Look for the hidden messages in what people say and signs around you to guide you to the truth you need.*
Zodiac: *Cancer.*
Empowerment: *There is time to spare if I do not squander it on worry.*

Magnesite

Type: Magnesium carbonate resembles chewing gum or a cauliflower floret.

Colours: Usually white, also marbled with grey, brown or tan.

Availability: Common.

Physical benefits: Alleged to be good for the gall bladder, stomach acidity, cholesterol, slowing down blood clotting, migraines, headaches, body odour, regulating extremes of body temperature, cramps and spasms, strong bones and teeth (as bracelet or necklace).

Emotional healing: Reduces intolerance of others, chronic irritability and dislike of children and animals.

Chakra: Brow and Crown.

Magnesite has been used for centuries as currency by Native North Americans. An excellent crystal for exhausted mothers if they have sleepless nights, it is also used in jewellery, dyed turquoise, as it has a similar texture to turquoise. Since magnesite opens Brow and Crown chakras, it is possible by closing your hands around four or five magnesites and focusing on a white candle flame to perceive higher realms. It is easily scratched so is best kept separate from other crystals.

Candle colour: *White.*

Fragrances: *Cherry blossom, lemon balm, lemon verbena, neroli, vanilla.*

Practical uses: *A very calming crystals; keep a small dish of white and /or dyed turquoise magnesite near food preparation and on the dining table.*

Magical significance: *Hold white magnesite against your brow, close your eyes and relax into a meditative state.*

Divinatory meaning: *Slow down, step back and what now seems insoluble will be manageable.*

Zodiac: *Libra.*

Empowerment: *All shall be well.*

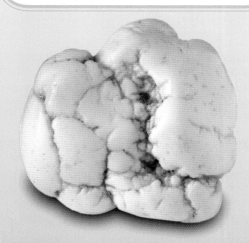

BANDED ONYX

Type: Quartz, chalcedony, a variety of agate, the white banded kind tends not to be heat-treated.

Colours: White with streaks of black, grey or cream; also varieties of orange, brown or green; white banded onyx is often found as broad bands with black onyx.

Availability: Common.

Physical benefits: Thought to help cells, particularly white blood cells, bone marrow, Hodgkinson's disease, lymph glands, thrush, vaginal infections, breasts, teeth, jaw, bone disorders, pregnancy, after a gynaecological or breast operation.

Emotional healing: Restores faith in people.

Chakra: Heart and Crown.

Banded onyx has long been used for ornamental purposes, especially cameos. Now there is a huge array of banded onyx, some dyed or heat-enhanced, some natural, but all equally powerful in its protective energies. White banded bowls enhance and cleanse crystals kept in them, while white or pale banded candle holders increase the luck-attracting and protective powers of the lighted flame. Drink your crystal elixirs from a white onyx cup to increase their potency.

Candle colour: *White.*

Fragrances: *Apple blossom, lily, lily of the valley, lotus, mimosa.*

Practical uses: *For mending lovers' quarrels; exchange matching small white banded onyx ornaments on your wedding or betrothal day.*

Magical significance: *Use a white onyx mortar and pestle for mixing herbs to empower them; before use, put your hands round it and ask that it be filled with light.*

Divinatory meaning: *Check with someone reliable what you have heard about your future.*

Zodiac: *Libra.*

Empowerment: *I seek highest motives in my words and actions.*

WHITE CORAL

Type: Organic, branching calcareous skeletons of sea creatures.

Colours: White, also red, orange, pink, blue and black.

Availability: Relatively common.

Physical benefits: Said to ease teething in infants, all children's illnesses, epilepsy, mobility; protect against falls in children and older people, female reproductive organs, scanty or absent menstruation, recovery from orthopaedic and microsurgery and for bone and cell regrowth, especially in older people; improve bone marrow, skin health, dry or inflamed skin, rashes, burns and scalds, acne, swollen scar tissue, digestion, stomach acidity, seasickness, arthritis in women; promote fertility,

Emotional healing: Overcomes fear of water in children and adults, and of travelling by sea; also for vertigo, particularly fears of falling from a great height.

Chakra: Sacral.

Candle colour: *White.*
Fragrances: *Lavender, lemon, lily, lily of the valley, mimosa.*
Practical uses: *Traditionally a coral and silver memento is given to the baby since coral protects the young and vulnerable.*
Magical significance: *White coral connects to water essences and spirits, especially those of the sea; a rare variety known as angel skin, because of its pink or peach tinge, is associated with Phul, angel of lakes and still waters; Rahab, angel of the ocean; Trsiel, the river angel; and Manakiel who protects dolphin, whales, seals and fish.*
Divinatory meaning: *What or who has gone will return when the time is right; do not fret for what cannot now be changed.*
Zodiac: *Pisces.*
Empowerment: *I accept loss and welcome gain as a two halves of the coin.*

Coral has been valued for years across many cultures, as a gift from the sea mothers, and is regarded as lucky, magical and protective, especially of children.
   White coral is linked with female goddess rituals and sacred sex magic (red coral may represent the male). The polished female white and a male natural red coral branch should be kept in a red bag beneath the bed when lovemaking, whether for a child or to increase passion.
   If coral breaks, its powers are no longer strong, so throw it back into the sea or any flowing water.

Milky Calcite

Type: Calcium carbonate.

Colours: Milky, cloudy white, softer and creamier than snow.

Availability: Common.

Physical benefits: Claimed to assist breast, tooth/gum problems, nursing mothers, osteoporosis/bone problems; pain; blood pressure, absorption of minerals especially calcium, negative energies; said to be antiseptic and gentle detoxifier.

Emotional healing: A mothering stone, for healing bad mothering experiences in adulthood, and helping new mothers to trust their instincts.

Chakra: Sacral and Heart.

Candle colour: *White or natural beeswax.*
Fragrances: *Apple blossom, lavender, lily, lily of the valley, neroli.*
Practical uses: *Absorbs bad vibes from quarrels or criticism; wash or smudge regularly.*
Magical significance: *To soothe noisy neighbours, place near a wall or fence. Hold each piece and say, "I bind you from disturbance and disruption with peace and blessings".*
Divinatory meaning: *Make peace with an old adversary but be vigilant.*
Zodiac: *Cancer.*
Empowerment: *I send healing to those in my life who are angry.*

In London's British Museum is an ornamental calcite seal from Mesopotamia, 3200–3000 BC.
  Milky white calcite was used widely in the ancient world – carved, as ritual bowls, and to keep food and drink pure. It is useful for past-life healing: sit by white candlelight or outdoors on a warm misty morning and let your mind drift. You may see images of why you have certain weaknesses; you can easily let them go. Even if you do not believe in past lives, this is a good healing exercise.

CLEAVELANDITE

Type: Silicate, plagioclase feldspar.

Colours: Creamy white to white to clear.

Availability: Relatively rare.

Physical benefits: Believed to assist with strokes, seizures, haemorrhaging and sudden brain malfunctions, Parkinson's disease and other tremors of limbs, dyspraxia, epilepsy, helps restore everyday connections after unconsciousness, amnesia.

Emotional healing: Assists academically advanced people to connect with other people and the world; for all who have chosen a solitary religious path or who are alone from choice to avoid total disconnection from life.

Chakra: Crown.

Candle colour: *White.*
Fragrances: *Bergamot, lemongrass, neroli, thyme, vanilla.*
Practical uses: *Bringing together two families on remarriage, particularly with twinned crystals.*
Magical significance: *The best stone for anyone after a near-death encounter or religious experience to return to everyday life yet retain positive insights and changes.*
Divinatory meaning: *Others may not share your dream but you may not have to leave them to fulfil it.*
Zodiac: *Aquarius.*
Empowerment: *I can walk seen and unseen worlds together.*

Cleavelandite is a bladed form of albite with long plated crystals that can grow large; as clusters it can form snowflake patterns and act as a matrix for crystals such as tourmaline. Excellent for journeying, spiritual or physical, and for putting far-reaching ideas into practice. In the home it brings contentment, soothing mid-life crises and encouraging change within existing relationships. If you find crystal-gazing difficult, focus on the whiteness of a large opaque white cleavelandite until images superimpose.

White Opal

Type: Hydrated silicon dioxide.

Colours: All precious opals with a light background are called white and have what is called a play of colours or inner fire of rainbow flashes in certain lights and when moved. Some white-coloured opals do not have opalescence.

Availability: Common.

Physical benefits: Claimed to balance left and right hemispheres of the brain; ease eyesight and visual disturbances, lactation in new mothers and infant feeding difficulties; help hormonal levels to return to normal after birth; regularize biorhythms; nervous system, nausea, fluid imbalances; aid menstrual difficulties at puberty.

Emotional healing: Alleviates food-related disorders by allowing the causes of poor self- and body-image to surface and be resolved; assists post-natal depression or failure to bond with an infant.

Chakra: Brow and Crown.

The rainbow colours in precious opals are made up of water and microscopic spheres of silica. As light rays are scattered by spaces between the spheres, they reflect from different levels in the stone.

White opals enhance beauty and inner radiance, and should be worn if you have lost confidence in yourself.

Use white opal to come to terms with life and find your true self; helpful to parents, particularly mothers experiencing empty-nest syndrome or women who have not worked outside the home and now want a job.

Candle colour: *White.*
Fragrances: *Almond, fig, mimosa, neroli, peach.*
Practical uses: *White opals are a symbol of lasting love on a very deep level and can be worn or given if an open permanent commitment is not possible between two lovers.*
Magical significance: *Wear white opal if learning yoga, Tai Chi and other gentle arts of spiritual movement, to merge with automatic subconscious levels of response so actions seem innate and natural rather than artificial and consciously learned.*
Divinatory meaning: *Persevere if a new activity or form of learning seems difficult: you will experience a breakthrough very soon.*
Zodiac: *Cancer.*
Empowerment: *I understand and respect my feelings.*

PEARL

Type: Organic, salt or freshwater.

Colours: White, grey, pale cream, pink/peach and blue, black, iridescent.

Availability: Common.

Physical benefits: Viewed as being good for skin, nausea and biliousness, fluid imbalances, bloating, hormones and PMS, fertility, female reproductive problems and sexuality, childbirth, digestion, soft organs and tissues, growths and tumours of all kinds.

Emotional healing: Pearls form a connection between our body rhythms and those of the natural cycles of the moon and the seasons, and so are very helpful for work-related burnout or stress overload and to prevent it recurring.

Chakra: Sacral and Heart.

Candle colour: *Silver.*
Fragrances: *Almond, apple blossom, magnolia, mimosa, peach.*
Practical uses: *Collect a pearl a year for a child. When the child is 18, the pearls can be made into a necklace for a young person or their future life partner, to give to the next generation.*
Magical significance: *Unthreading a string of broken pearls will loosen the psychological hold of a destructive or over-dominant person in your life; have the pearls restrung in a new way, perhaps adding new ones to strengthen your own identity.*
Divinatory meaning: *You may have considered a lot of unpromising offers recently but keep looking, for the right opportunity is close.*
Zodiac: *Cancer.*
Empowerment: *Good fortune surrounds me.*

Pearls form when an oyster swallows an irritant such as grain of sand, and then coats it with nacre – calcium carbonate, which it deposits in concentric layers that build up the pearl. Pearls may be natural (saltwater or freshwater) or cultured, the latter grown by introducing the irritant into the oyster.

Healing and metaphysical energies are virtually the same for both forms. Natural pearls are rare and very precious. Pearls from the sea are valued most highly.

BPearls represent integrity, especially if white or cream. In the home they encourage tradition, particularly in the form of a necklace, an unbroken circle. Keep with family photographs or records such as birth certificates.

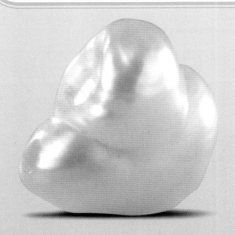

GRAPHITE

Type: Carbon, native element.

Colours: Silvery grey, black.

Availability: Common.

Physical benefits: May be helpful for feet, ankles, legs, spine, bowel and large intestine, for any physical blockages in the lower half of the body, constipation.

Emotional healing: Any form of post-traumatic stress, especially if resulting in disability or memory loss; for sudden uprooting of children from a familiar home.

Chakra: Root.

Graphite and diamond both consist of the element carbon, yet are very different. Graphite is soft, shiny grey and used in pencils. Diamond, meanwhile, is a colourless sparkling gem, the hardest mineral.
   The properties of graphite make the mineral valuable metaphysically: as a focus for expressing knowledge and ideas clearly and creatively, and for removing resistance to gently let disappear what is no longer needed or is destructive in a person's life.
   Keep graphite in quartz with your healthy-eating plan when dieting as a reminder of the person you are releasing; each time you lose half a kilo, write your new weight on paper in pencil and rub the old weight out.
   Graphite protects against electrical faults, fires and electrocution at home or work. Lie with a small piece on each knee to remove old sorrow and to balance your inner energy system.

Candle colour: *Grey.*
Fragrances: *Cedar, clary sage, vetivert.*
Practical uses: *A Mother Earth crystal, graphite is a good addition to the home if money is short to get value for money in transactions; also to encourage thriftiness and creative alternatives to expensive outings and designer items.*
Magical use: *To get rid of something harmful from your life, take a new pencil and write what you wish to lose very faintly on white or grey paper; rub graphite gently over the writing, then use an eraser to remove the writing. Burn the blank paper.*
Divinatory meaning: *Sometimes what is useful is of more value than what is attractive, so do not be taken in by appearances.*
Zodiac: *Capricorn*
Empowerment: *I value quality and not cost.*

Molybdenite

Type: Sulphide, soft enough to leave a mark on paper and fingers.

Colours: Steel grey, bluish silver, metallic (looks similar to graphite but lighter and bluer).

Availability: Rare.

Physical benefits: Thought to promote strength and vitality by rebalancing the body in all its functions; for circulation, teeth, jaw and face problems; assist if you have mercury fillings, with detoxification; immune system, soft tissues and ligaments.

Emotional healing: Used for retrieving buried memories to explain and release phobias or seemingly illogical fears; recovering or developing your true personality and potential if you have spent your life trying to please others.

Chakra: Brow.

Candle colour: *Silver.*
Fragrances: *Galbanum, geranium, magnolia, mimosa, mugwort.*
Practical uses: *Keep close when writing letters or emails when you have to disappoint someone or break some bad news about a change in plans.*
Magical significance: *To get answers to questions in a dream, write your question on paper, rub molybdenite on the paper over the writing, fold the paper and put near your bed, reciting the question softly till you fall asleep.*
Divinatory meaning: *Listen to your dreams, especially recurring ones as they are warning you about a person or situation where you are shutting your mind to the truth.*
Zodiac: *Aquarius.*
Empowerment: *Dreams are for living.*

Molybdenite contains one of the rarest elements in the Earth's crust, rhenium. The crystal itself is often found attached to a quartz matrix, which amplifes its energies.

The dreamer's stone, it helps with all forms of dream work. Place it near your bed for creative and peaceful sleep and to overcome any sleep disorders. In waking hours, it can be used in meditation to see ourselves from within and to identify unhelpful influences in our lives.

Molybdenite will, if gently held close to the Heart chakra in the centre of the breast or chest, release healing for any physical or emotional problems. It is a soft crystal, so needs to be handled carefully and is not suitable for elixirs.

HAEMATITE

Type: Iron oxide, harder than iron.

Colours: Metallic grey, silver, black. Availability: Common. Physical benefits: Said to help with blood disorders, particularly of red cells, the absorption of iron and other minerals, blood clots, circulation, energy levels, fatigue, backache, travel sickness particularly by air, jet lag; function as a pain remover and reduce excessive bleeding, whether from a wound, during menstruation or in childbirth.

Emotional healing: Relieves fears of seeing blood, obsessions about contagious illnesses; over-sensitivity to bodily functions particularly using toilets not your own; fears of flying and of insects, especially spiders.

Chakra: Root.

All haematite has a rusty red streak that can be seen when it is powdered or when natural haematite is rubbed against a harder stone.

Its name in Ancient Greek means "blood" because it was believed the stone bled if scratched. Indeed, in Neolithic times, bones were interred with powdered haematite to represent the blood of Mother Earth. As a magnetic stone, haematite will draw success to you. If you do not normally take credit for your achievements, wearing haematite jewellery will bring you praise and tangible rewards, such as a rise in salary or promotion for what was previously overlooked. Matching haematite (for Mars) set in copper (for Venus) can be worn by a couple as a sign of commitment.

If you have a pacemaker, it is not advisable to wear or carry haematite.

Candle colour: *Silver.*
Fragrances: *Allspice, basil, dragon's blood, poppy, thyme.*
Practical uses: *Called the lawyer's stone. Carry haematite for success in court; also for any DIY legal work, to ensure you are clear, concise and not swayed by pressure.*
Magical significance: *Polished haematite was used as magic mirrors to foresee the future. These mirrors were used both for divination and in magic spells to reflect back hostility to the sender. Gaze within a flat piece of polished haematite, a haematite sphere or egg by candlelight to see your guides.*
Divinatory meaning: *Someone pressurizing you to change your mind or make concessions has no real authority; ignore this petty bullying.*
Zodiac: *Aries.*
Empowerment: *I will not give way to unfair pressure.*

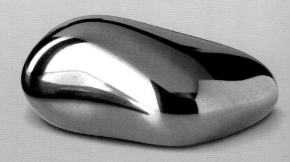

METEORITE

Type: Magnetic space rock, alloyed with nickel and iron.

Colours: Grey, black, brown-black or red-brown on outside, often silver-grey inside.

Availability: Some rare, some relatively common.

Physical benefits: May help with muscle spasms, muscular tension, stomach cramps, digestive system; illness difficult to diagnose or treatment slow to show results, head or brain disorder, injury or pain, eye problems such as squints or cataracts, facial disfigurement.

Emotional healing: Keeps feet firmly on the ground when caught up in heady emotional attachments or sudden temptations later regretted.

Chakra: Root and Solar Plexus.

Candle colour: *Silver.*

Fragrances: *Frankincense, grapefruit, lime, myrrh, sandalwood.*

Practical uses: *Place meteorite around the home near entrances, to protect from fire or attack. Carry meteorite as an amulet against international terrorism, bombs, hijacking or violent crime, especially involving guns or knives.*

Magical significance: *A stone for those involved in astrology or cryptozoology; helpful for any who have experienced alien encounters in dreams or more directly.*

Divinatory meaning: *You may need to leave preconceptions behind when dealing with an unusual situation or person with a totally different life view.*

Zodiac: *All signs, especially Aquarius and Scorpio.*

Empowerment: *There is a universe of experience to discover.*

Most meteorites originate in the asteroid belt between Mars and Jupiter, where there are many rock fragments. One of the most common small spherical meteorites, chondrite, is unchanged since the solar system was formed and unlike any rocks on Earth.

Meteorites have been used since ancient times: the Egyptians capped some of their pyramids with them. The Black Stone at Mecca is a meteorite, said by Islamic tradition to have been sent from Heaven to show Adam and Eve where to build the first temple on Earth.

Whether we believe in extra-terrestrial life or not, meteorites bring messages from the cosmos to help us to make the world a better place in small personal ways. Good for taking the first steps towards a more fulfilling way of life.

BLACK OBSIDIAN

Type: Volcanic glass/magma, formed when lava hardens so fast that no crystalline structures are created.

Colours: Black and gleaming.

Availability: Common.

Physical benefits: Claimed to assist with pain relief; improve circulation and artery health, also bowel problems. Thought to be useful to recover from physical shock, whether after an accident, an operation, or trauma.

Emotional healing: Emotional healing after trauma of any kind. Good for victims of sexual assault. Assists in expressing grief that is blocked, especially in children. A small obsidian sphere in your workspace and at home absorbs free-floating irritability and restlessness.

Chakra: Root.

Called the wizard stone, obsidian has magical associations. Highly polished obsidian oracle mirrors were used by the Mayans and Aztecs. The seven obsidian arrow heads of the Ancient Egyptian lion-headed goddess Sekhmet were sent against wrongdoers.

Set seven-pointed obsidian arrow crystals in a semi-circle round your workspace or round a burgundy candle, facing inwards, to draw power and health into yourself. Use to call for employment or a better job.

Obsidian beneath a pet's bed will make a nervous pet less sensitive to being touched or sudden noises.

Obsidian tends to be a very personal stone and is generally bought, kept and worn by one person only.

Candle colour: *Bergundy*

Fragrances: *Benzoin, gum arabic (acacia), mint, parsley, pine, pine resin (pinon or collophony), sandalwood.*

Practical uses: *Protective when carried or worn as jewellery if others offload their problems on to you or make excessive demands on your time.*

Divinatory meaning: *You have a great deal of power that you can use to improve a situation or relationship if you are not afraid to change the status quo and maybe tread on a few toes.*

Zodiac: *Scorpio.*

Empowerment: *I am filled with fire.*

LODESTONE

Type: Naturally magnetized iron oxide, sometimes classed as a metal. The male stones are pointed, the female square or rounded. Buy a pair, one of each.

Colours: Black, dark grey, occasionally light brown.

Availability: Found in specialist crystal stores and online.

Physical benefits: Use male lodestones for men and female for women: believed to assist with arthritis, rheumatism, muscle aches, cramps, pain relief, circulation blockages, heartbeat, impotence, bowels, rectum, lower back, eyes, soles of feet.

Emotional healing: Hold your lodestone pair, one on each hand as seems right, each morning to feel long-standing burdens lift and helplessness be replaced by self-reliance.

Chakra: Root and Solar Plexus.

Candle colour: *Red.*
Fragrances: *Basil, bay, juniper, red rose, thyme.*
Practical uses: *Keep a pair at home in a red bag to ensure balanced energies flowing in and out and reduce geopathic stress from negative earth energies; good to stop opposite-sex siblings from arguing.*
Magical significance: *A male and female lodestone, or two the same for same-sex relationships, are traditionally kept in a red bag to maintain faithful love.*
Divinatory meaning: *Follow your instincts.*
Zodiac: *Virgo, Libra and Capricorn.*
Empowerment: *I am tuned in to my radar.*

Lodestones have been used to symbolically draw luck, money and love. In healing, a painful place or source of an illness would be stroked in downward movements and afterwards the stone placed in water and the water thrown away; rub a rounded stone in circles over the body if muscles are tense or for aches and pains. A pair beneath the mattress of a marital bed preserves passion and helps conceive a child; traditionally a male lodestone is anointed on the night of the full moon with a drop of patchouli to increase male potency (wash next morning).

BLACK TIGER'S EYE

Type: Quartz embedded in crocidolite with little of the hydrated oxide that gives tiger's eye its customary golden colour; very dark form of hawk's or falcon's eye (blue).

Colours: Black or very dark blue, also includes darker greys, sometimes dyed.

Availability: Rarest form of tiger's eye.

Physical benefits: Believed to provide help for all slow-moving degenerative conditions, to trigger the body's natural resistance, deep-seated tumours or growths anywhere, particularly in men, prostate, hernia, bowels, large intestine and anus in both sexes, internal bleeding for example from an ulcer, deep vein thrombosis, mental and physical blackouts whatever the cause.

Emotional healing: A stone for men who have suffered a severe emotional or psychological setback, such as the loss of a lifetime partner through death or desertion, redundancy in later life and no prospect of re-employment or a financial disaster, to work through grief and anger and rebuild their lives step by step in a new way.

Chakra: Root.

This unusual tiger's eye is heavier in its energies than its brother, the hawk's or falcon's eye. Sometimes called the impenetrable fortress stone, it ensures that anything unhelpful bounces back with triple the force it was sent with and galvanizes the body and mind's defences.

Black tiger's eye is protects and empowers anyone serving in the armed forces on the front line, to focus on their strengths and loyalties to one another.

Associated candle colour: *Dark grey.*

Associated fragrances: *Anise, cloves, grapefruit, lime and tea tree.*

Practical uses: *The toughest of the tiger's eyes. Wear as jewellery at difficult times to give you the resilience not to give in to adversity; touch in the darkest hours to push towards the light.*

Magical significance: *The ultimate shield to reflect back hostility and to protect you against psychic vampires. If you know you will be meeting a draining or nasty person, touch your brow, your throat and your heat with the stone to seal your main chakra or psychic-energy centre weak-points.*

Divinatory meaning: *If the odds seem stacked against you, keep pushing: a week or two will see you through the other side.*

Zodiac: *Scorpio.*

Empowerment: *I overcome adversity with courage.*

LARVAKITE

Type: Black feldspar.

Colours: Black-grey, blue-grey, grey, all with sheen or iridescent colour flashes, often of silvery blue.

Availability: Found in specialist crystal stores and online. Physical benefits: Said to help high blood pressure, brain functioning, recovery after strokes and thrombosis, brain stem, intellect, congested lungs, PMS, menopausal hot flushes, skin.

Emotional healing: Encourages rationality; ideal for hormonal teenagers, pregnancy, perimenopausal mood swings and passionate new lovers.

Chakra: Base, Throat, Brow, Crown.

Larvikite, or Norwegian moonstone, is an igneous rock that is mined in Norway, named after the local town of Larvik. It is useful for activating those with grand dreams who are going to start tomorrow. Larvikite has grounding energies to connect with nature and counteract over-exposure to artificial stimulants, over-bright lighting and constant background noise. It brings psychic dreams, connecting with ancestors, spirit guides and past lives, and aids recall and understanding of dream messages. Brings healing during sleep.

Candle colour: *Blue or silver.*
Fragrances: *Myrrh, poppy, rosemary, sage, sweetgrass.*
Practical uses: *Carry if you are learning new skills; you have to combine learning with work or caring for a family, if you are under financial pressure or face opposition to your studies.*
Magical significance: *Reverses spells; wear to neutralize nasty wishes and consign them to the cosmos for transformation.*
Divinatory meaning: *Do not part with money unless you are sure the person asking has a genuine need and will pay you back.*
Zodiac: *Leo and Sagittarius.*
Empowerment: *I open my heart wisely.*

LABORADITE

Type: Plagioclase feldspar.

Colours: Grey-green, dark grey, black or grey-white with flashes of blue, red, gold, orange, purple and green.

Availability: Common.

Physical benefits: May help bronchitis, respiratory complaints, lungs, metabolism, colds, digestion, eyes, brain disorders, PMS, menstruation, warts, skin and hair parasites, gout, rheumatism, high blood pressure, pain relief.

Emotional healing: For reducing anti-social, reckless or impulsive behaviour in children, teenagers and adults who are easily led into trouble by others.

Chakra: Brow and Root.

Candle colour: *Blue.*
Fragrances: *Cedar, copal, dragon's blood, juniper, lemongrass.*
Practical uses: *Wear laboradite to stay neutral and if you are caught in the centre of a dispute and are asked to take sides or pass judgment on other's actions.*
Magical significance: *Provides a powerful entry-point tool in developing clairvoyant vision; turn a laboradite sphere, egg or polished pebble round fast so it catches the light and the colours merge and separate into rainbow images.*
Divinatory meaning: *You may have to temporarily make the best of a less-than-ideal situation, but soon you will be able to do things your way.*
Zodiac: *Scorpio.*
Empowerment: *I can be both independent and connected with others.*

Laboradite was discovered by Moravian missionaries to North America in 1770. Inuit peoples speak of a legend according to which an Inuit warrior struck the stone with his spear and created the Northern Lights.

When light hits the stone it is refracted on the different layers formed during crystallization, which produces laboradite 's characteristic and iridescent colouring. Wearing laboradite brings the fun and spontaneity back into your life if you are stuck in routine or weighed down by responsibility; it awakens a sense of adventure, sometimes for the first time.

A stone of independent thought and action, so keep laboradite with papers or near computer files you are checking to avoid making errors or missing incorrect facts that have been inserted in a document.

PURPLE SPINEL

Type: Magnesium aluminium oxide. Spinels made artificially are not so good for healing or empowerment.

Colours: Purple from light to dark violet, including lavender.

Availability: Relatively common.

Physical benefits: Said to be a whole-body healer if placed in the centre of the brow; remove deep-seated pain; relieve epilepsy, migraines, hardening of arteries in brain, hydrocephalus, Parkinson's disease, motor neurone disease, paralysis of lower body, circulatory problems in legs, skin and hair health; detoxify blood.

Emotional healing: Reduces a sense of isolation from any social group, whether colleagues, family or the community; wear if you are disabled to find the resources to overcome practical difficulties and ignorance in others.

Chakra: Brow.

Purple spinel combines spirituality with the dynamic regenerative powers of spinel; good therefore for launching a spiritual business as a second career so that it provides a living. It protects against everyday nastiness and paranormal harm, acting as a shield to reflect back ill wishes without amplifying them or sending anything harmful in return.

   Wear purple spinel as jewellery to maintain your own ethics if you have to associate with cynical, materialistic people or if you are trying to fit in with people who have very different beliefs. Purple spinel reassures older people confused by the modern world.

Candle colour: *Purple.*
Fragrances: *Acacia, copal, hydrangea, juniper, sage.*
Practical uses: *An intergenerational harmony stone; give to older relations to encourage independence, but as a reassurance that you are there if necessary; keep natural spinel in your home to create a sense of space and personal boundaries if your living space is crowded.*
Magical significance: *Draws to you and at the same time guides you to like-minded people who share your spiritual outlook and interests.*
Divinatory meaning: *You have the interests of others at heart; since your current decision does involve them, consider their needs, but do not forget your own first.*
Zodiac: *Scorpio and Pisces.*
Empowerment: *I can find the best in any situation.*

AMETHYST

Type: Purple form of crystallized quartz; the colour comes from the presence of manganese during its formation.

Colours: Pale lilac and lavender to deep purple, also purple and white.

Availability: Common.

Physical benefits: Called the all-healer of people, animals and plants; this is believed to benefit migraines and headaches if you rub the forehead anti-clockwise, having dipped the amethyst in running water.

Emotional healing: "Amethystos" meant not to be intoxicated in Ancient Greek, and amethyst reduces addiction, obsessive compulsive disorder, hyperactivity in children and animals; called nature's tranquillizer.

Chakra: Brow.

Candle colour: *Any shade of purple.*
Fragrances: *Acacia, almond, lavender, fern, lily.*
Practical uses: *Amethyst counteracts negative earth energies beneath a building; place amethyst near where plants will not grow or animals refuse to sit; use natural unpolished amethysts or geodes.*
Magical significance: *Protects against paranormal harm or ill-wishing and attracts good luck. Draw a sun image and the crescent moon over an amethyst in lavender incense smoke for both powers.*
Divinatory meaning: *I do not need to reward myself any excesses of any kind to feel good.*
Zodiac: *Aquarius.*
Empowerment: *I can control my cravings.*

Amethyst was worn by the first Christians. It is the stone of St Valentine and of faithful lovers, because St Valentine is believed to have worn an amethyst ring engraved with an image of Cupid. Wear as a ring for fidelity or as a locket to call back lost love.

An unpolished amethyst in the bedroom guards against nightmares and insomnia: rub anti-clockwise in the centre of the forehead, just above and between the eyes, the seat of the Third Eye. It helps to protect against homesickness.

Placed in the centre of the brow, it aids meditation and visualization; keep unpolished amethyst near other crystals to recharge them.

CHAROITE

Type: Phyllo or sheet silicate.

Colours: Purple, lilac and violet in swirling patterns.

Availability: Rare. The only place in the world it can be found is in the Chary River in Russia.

Physical benefits: Thought to improve cramps, high blood pressure, migraines, sleep problems including sleepwalking and sleep-talking, autism and Asperger's syndrome, ADHD.

Emotional healing: Fear of ill-health, pain and dying; acute loneliness and alienation from life and other people.

Chakra: Crown.

Because charoite comes from an area of Siberia once associated with political prisoners, it has become a symbol of endurance and comfort in adversity; gives the courage to start over after repossession, for job loss in an area of high unemployment, for anyone in prison or in residential care; from boarding school to hospital.

A carers' crystal when nursing the sick or elderly and for adoptive parents to bond with children with behavioural difficulties. Wear charoite to prevent premonitions of disasters you cannot prevent, and to channel these powers into positive intuition.

Candle colour: *Lilac.*
Fragrances: *Lavender, lilac and musk.*
Practical uses: *For people who work away from home to maintain connection with their home, and for those who live alone and have little contact with others*
Magical significance: *Strengthens telepathic bonds. Hold a tumblestone, close your eyes, picture the person you wish to contact and speak to them.*
Divinatory meaning: *News of an old friend or love and a chance to make a positive connection.*
Zodiac: *Pisces.*
Empowerment: *I can feel at home anywhere.*

TANZANITE AURA

Type: Silicate, quartz, treated with gold, niobium and indium at exceedingly high temperatures, giving it a permanent metallic sheen.

Colours: Indigo. It is slightly paler than its sky-blue cousin aqua aura.

Availability: Relatively rare, but so beautiful it is worth seeking out.

Physical benefits: Assists all problems of the head and neck, including thyroid glands, vision, memory, mental faculties; good for memory loss and for halting age-related effects on the mind, dysfunctional neural functions, epilepsy, helpful for brain damage after strokes, accident or viral infections.

Emotional healing: Good for releasing negativity that has built up over in a mentally abusive relationship; also good for anyone who has suffered violent crime.

Chakra: Crown, Brow, Throat and Heart.

Candle colour: *Purple.*
Fragrances: *Cherry blossom, lavender, lily, Solomon's seal and thyme.*
Practical uses: *Helps adults and children who have learning difficulties or multiple disabilities and for anyone with Down's Syndrome to achieve their full potential.*
Magical significance: *A relatively new angel crystal that brings connection with Raziel the Archangel of mysteries and all esoteric knowledge. Hold tanzine aura and ask Raziel to remove bad karma holding you back from happiness.*
Divinatory meaning: *Time is running short, but you will be offered what you have asked or applied for, or something as good.*
Zodiac: *Sagittarius and Capricorn.*
Empowerment: *There is always a way to fix things.*

A crystal of many names (such as tanzanite aura, tanzan aura or indigo aura), tanzine aura helps us to connect to our inner source of knowledge and the Akashic wisdom of humankind everywhere; improves intuition in the everyday world as well as spiritually; brings the earthly and spiritual worlds closer to recognize and express our true qualities for success with integrity.

A valuable crystal for mediums, especially for those looking for evidence acceptable to the scientific community of psychic powers and life after death.

Azurite

Type: Copper carbonate with high copper content, occasionally with a copper sheen.

Colours: Bright azure blue usually mixed with dark blue.

Availability: Common.

Physical benefits: May be useful for spine and rib-cage disorders, circulation, oxygenating the blood, brain-cell repair; for Alzheimer's, dementia and other degenerative brain-related disorders and for easing conditions related to ageing; detoxifying the system.

Emotional healing: Excellent for overcoming an inferiority complex, living only to please others and domestic bullying, whether by your children, partners, parents or friends who always know best.

Chakra: Throat and Brow.

Candle colour: *Bright blue.*
Fragrances: *Clary sage, lotus, orchid, sagebrush, sandalwood.*
Practical uses: *At home azurite lessens tensions between different generations, especially when sharing a home with three or more generations; for harmoniously bringing together different sets of grandparents and relations in the lives of families involved in step-parenting.*
Magical significance: *A stone for connecting with sacred powers through religious music, such as Gregorian or Buddhist chants, choral music and hymns; also for healing using sound, especially drums, the didgeridoo, pipes and the voice.*
Divinatory meaning: *Look to the long-term advantages and not immediate gain or results.*
Zodiac: *Sagittarius.*
Empowerment: *I can be noble in victory and defeat.*

The Ancient Chinese called azurite the stone of heaven because they believed it opened celestial gateways. The Ancient Egyptians used the pigment to paint the protective eye of Horus, the sky god, on their foreheads.

Azurite is a good crystal for older people living alone or in sheltered accommodation to maintain their independence, mental alertness and physical health.

A stone to encourage study and concentration for older school children and college students; especially helpful for mature students to fit in study with other commitments; encourages study during retirement and also travel and relocating abroad for the over-fifties. A natural long-term prosperity bringer.

AQUAMARINE

Type: Beryl, ring silicate.

Colours: Clear light blue, blue-green or aqua. The deeper and purer the blue, the more valuable the aquamarine.

Availability: Common.

Physical benefits: Said to be useful for throat infections and voice loss, teeth and gum problems, bladder, kidneys, cystitis, lymph glands and fluid retention, colds, bronchitis and other upper respiratory difficulties, body and mouth odour, sunburn; helpful in hot climates to keep cool.

Emotional healing: Calms perpetually angry or bad-tempered people, mood swings and excessive toddler and teenage tantrums, heals the effects of over-judgemental parents who set impossible standards and panic attacks that linger as guilt and inadequacy in adulthood.

Chakra: Throat and Heart.

Associated candle colour: *Aquamarine.*
Practical uses: *Since aquamarine's power is enhanced by water, aquamarine elixir – water in which tumbled aquamarine has been soaked for a few hours – is good for sore throats; will help prevent motion sickness; and can be used in drinks to bring calm and prompt kind words.*
Magical significance: *Attracts and keeps good luck and love with you if worn or carried; leave aquamarine in moonlight on the night of the full moon and sprinkle it the next morning with water also left overnight in moonlight, to recharge its talismanic powers.*
Divinatory meaning: *Go with what is on offer rather than waiting for the ideal opportunity or time.*
Zodiac: *Pisces*
Empowerment: *I open my heart to forgiveness.*

Its name from the Latin aqua marinus, 'water of the sea', refers to its ocean-like colour. Aquamarine protects sailors and all who travel by or over water and minimizes travel delays; is good when learning to swim; and prevents love quarrels, increases commitment and preserves fidelity so long as the waters of the earth flow.

  A stone of justice through negotiation, so pass it over any written complaints you receive or before you send them; wear or carry aquamarine before seeking to resolve disputes. Touch the stone and say, "May wise justice prevail." If you normally avoid confrontation, it will give you courage and clear reasoned words.

TANZANITE

Type: Variety of zoisite, epidote (calcium aluminium silicate).

Colours: Blue to blue-violet.

Availability: Becoming rarer and more valuable, as supply is expected to dry up in around 15 years.

Physical benefits: Said to strengthen the immune system; detoxify the body and improve vitality; promote the regeneration of cells, skin and hair; preserve youthfulness; protect against the side-effects of medical or surgical intervention.

Emotional healing: Calming and soothing, even a tiny piece of tanzanite is good for adults to overcome communication difficulties.

Chakra: Third Eye or Brow Chakra, Crown and Throat.

Tanzanite was discovered in 1967 at the foot of Mount Kilimanjaro in Tanzania (hence the name). Popular legend regards tanzanite as a gift from the gods, since it was discovered by Masai cattle herders who saw the blue stones after brown zoisite crystals on the ground were burned in a bush fire caused by lightning.Indeed, some tanzanite on sale is heat-treated brown zoisite.
  Tanzanite is excellent to wear if you are beginning to explore your psychic powers, as it enables your clairvoyant Brow chakra to open gradually so you are not overwhelmed. Circle tanzanite clockwise in the centre of your brow to open your third eye and psychic powers, and anti-clockwise to close it so you can relax.

Candle colour: *Blue or purple.*
Fragrances: *Lemon verbena, lilac, mimosa, vanilla, violet.*
Practical uses: *Helps bring out the other side of your personality; if, for example, you are normally serious, you will discover quite spontaneously your fun side emerging.*
Magical significance: *Meditate while holding this crystal to make contact with your spirit guides and to connect with deceased loved ones, especially in the early days after the bereavement.*
Divinatory meaning: *Trust your intuition – it is guiding you in the right direction, even though others may be blinding you with facts and figures to the contrary.*
Zodiac: *Gemini, Libra and Sagittarius.*
Empowerment: *My hidden abilities unfold in unexpected ways.*

LAPIS LAZULI

Type: Rock, formed by multiple minerals including lazurite, sodalite, calcite and pyrite.

Colours: Rich medium to royal blue, purple-blue, green-blue with gold flecks (pyrites).

Availability: Relatively common.

Physical benefits: May help with the endocrine and nervous systems, headaches, migraines, lymph glands, bone marrow, ears and nasal passages; reduce pain and inflammation; believed to be good for autism or Asperger's syndrome.

Emotional healing: Helps take responsibility for self, rather than blaming others for missed opportunities.

Chakra: Throat and Brow.

Lapis lazuli has been mined in the mountains of Afghanistan for 6,000 years, and was amongst the first gemstones to be used as jewellery. Lapis Lazuli is a stone of truth, encouraging truth in the spoken and written word and honesty in the spirit.

Wear it for all forms of deep communication, for example when you have a heart-to-heart with a loved one. Lapis lazuli is also considered a stone of friendship and can help bring about harmony in any relationship and make it long-lasting.

Candle colour: *Blue or gold.*
Fragrances: *Cyphi, geranium, lotus, magnolia, orchid.*
Practical uses: *If you want fame, wear or carry lapis lazuli to auditions*
Magical significance: *Place lapis in the centre of your brow to open your Third Eye.*
Divinatory meaning: *It is the right time to get yourself noticed in a positive way: a high-profile presentation of your talents is the key.*
Zodiac: *Virgo and Libra*
Empowerment: *I reach for the stars.*

Blue Jasper

Type: Silicate, microcrystalline quartz, often with organic matter or other minerals as inclusions.

Colours: Various shades of blue, often with darker patches or veins; can be artificially treated to accentuate the blue.

Availability: One of the rarer jaspers.

Physical benefits: Thought to encourage recovery from trauma, severe accident or a major illness where a person has to learn to live again; recovery of speech faculties and relearning language after a stroke or accident; the relief of post-traumatic stress syndrome; recovery from brain and eye surgery; assist with problems of ageing.

Emotional healing: Called the warrior stone, jasper in its blue shades strengthens self-determination in a fight against an addiction that has proved resistant to therapy and rehabilitation.

Chakra: Throat and Brow.

Blue jasper brings the courage of one's convictions to speak out against injustice and risk unpopularity; a stone for making a difference through charitable ventures; let older children carry blue jasper to resist being led into unwise behaviour to gain popularity.

A tiny blue jasper on an animal collar prevents smaller animals being bullied and deters aggressors.

Blue jasper is linked with nobility of purpose; wear it if you work in a situation where others are less than honest. Keep it at home to teach children how to tell the truth without being hurtful, for blue jasper represents honesty with kindness.

Candle colour: *Dark blue.*
Fragrances: *Benzoin, bergamot, lemon, lemongrass, myrrh.*
Practical uses: *A stone for studying any subject with a lot of facts, particularly if you have to combine study with work or other responsibilities.*
Magical significance: *Hold a piece of blue jasper jewellery if you seek a mentor to help in your career or learning path; wear the jewellery during sleep, quiet contemplation and while studying.*
Divinatory meaning: *You may need to decide how far to help someone close who is in trouble without making things too hard for yourself.*
Zodiac: *Sagittarius.*
Empowerment: *I speak the truth without fear.*

BLUE WERNERITE

Type: Silicate; wernerite is the old name used for the mineral.

Colours: Pale to rich blue, sometimes with pyrite specks.

Availability: Found in specialist mineral stores and online.

Physical benefits: Believed to help with veins and arteries, high blood pressure, circulation overload, nervous breakdown, stiff neck or swollen neck glands, glandular fever, Hodgkin's lymphoma, headaches caused by tension, toothache and gum health, persistent ear infections.

Emotional healing: Prevents us sabotaging our own efforts to break free of bad habits and then blaming others or circumstances; assists in taking responsibility..

Chakra: Throat.

Blue wernerite (also called scapolite) brings a calm response to any challenge; removes irritability and encourages a balanced reaction to apparent injustice. Use if you are building up expertise. Wear if you are applying for a leadership position or want to start your own enterprise to get resources; good also for expansion into a business partnership with someone whose skills complement your own or for developing two separate but parallel careers which eventually you can merge into a larger venture. Helps all shared ventures.

Candle colour: *Sky blue.*
Fragrances: *Eucalyptus, lavender, lily, rosemary, vanilla.*
Practical uses: *A stone to encourage children to persevere in learning new skills; give to those leaving the nest to encourage self-reliance.*
Magical significance: *A crystal for connecting with angels and spirit guides through written messages; place on a bible, book of poetry or sacred writings, focus on a question, hold in one hand and open the book anywhere with the other; run crystal down page until you feel you have reached the message and read.*
Divinatory meaning: *You know more than you realize.*
Zodiac: *Libra.*
Empowerment: *I know the answer.*

TURQUOISE

Type: Phosphate with traces of copper and iron.

Colours: Blue-green, sometimes mottled.

Availability: Quite rare and highly prized if natural and untreated; otherwise widely obtainable and often found as jewellery.

Physical benefits: Assists in dealing with problems of the brain, eyes, ears, neck and throat, respiratory and lung disorders, viral infections, migraines and headaches, allergies such as hay fever, arthritis, rheumatism and problems with balance.

Emotional healing: Calms the mind and eases depression; for jet lag and fears of flying; good for empowering yourself if you feel a victim or suffer prejudice or bullying.

Chakra: Throat.

Candle colour: *Blue or green.*
Fragrances: *Cedar, honeysuckle, pine, sage, sandalwood.*
Practical uses: *Overcomes writer's block, attached to a collar, bridle or cage; turquoise prevents animals straying or being stolen and makes horses sure-footed and obedient to their riders.*
Magical significance: *A stone of wisdom, to access knowledge from your unconscious mind and what has been called by the 20th-century psychotherapist Jung the collective unconscious of humanity in all times and places.*
Divinatory meaning: *A need for honesty and clearing up misunderstandings to set you free.*
Zodiac: *Sagittarius and Capricorn*
Empowerment: *I will not fail or fall.*

Turquoise has been prized for thousands of years as a symbol of wisdom, nobility and the power of immortality, among the Ancient Egyptians, Aztecs, the Native North Americans and the Ancient Chinese. The death mask of Tutankhamum was studied with turquoise, and for Moctezuma, the last ruler of the Aztecs, the stone was a symbol of his power and wealth, symbolizind his position as a deity.

Worn as jewellery or carried in a pouch, turquoise is a talisman for immense good luck, success, money, fame, ambition and creativity.

Above all a crystal of justice, both for obtaining it through the legal system and for fair and equal treatment in every area of life.

COBALT AURA

Type: Molecules of pure cobalt bonded by a natural electric charge to clear quartz.

Colours: Brilliant shades of metallic blue, violet and gold mixed.

Availability: Found in specialist crystal stores and online.

Physical benefits: Believed to help combine the body's own self-healing powers with higher healing; help if illness is unresponsive to treatment or a patient is exhausted by prolonged medical intervention, absorption of vitamins and minerals, functioning of enzymes, kidneys, pancreas, liver, spleen, myelin sheath; processing of glucose.

Emotional healing: Even a small piece of opens doors and both calms and inspires agoraphobics.

Chakra: Throat.

Cobalt aura is one of the generations of New Age crystals, created from natural minerals using the best of modern techniques, to join the old and new worlds in harmony. They contain natural minerals and elements, and so can be used for healing as well as empowerment and protection; indeed, they gain powers the separate components do not possess.

Cobalt aura increases natural clairvoyance and healing powers; a cluster held regularly will ease the transition between personal spiritual work and formal training or turning professional. Aids creative cooking.

Candle colour: *Sky blue.*
Fragrances: *Almond, cedarwood, lemon, lime.*
Practical uses: *Makes every day seem special; even a small cluster in the home removes restlessness and discontentment.*
Magical significance: *Like other combined aura crystals, cobalt aura brings special moments of joy.*
Divinatory meaning: *A good time for redecorating your home.*
Zodiac: *Sagittarius.*
Empowerment: *I will bring more colour into my daily world.*

EMERALD

Type: Beryl.

Colours: Bright green.

Availability: Common.

Physical benefits: May be useful for angina, eyesight, bleeding, epilepsy, fevers, fertility and childbirth, asthma, bronchitis and respiratory complaints, heart, thyroid, lungs, plant allergies, glands, teeth, kidneys and bladder, insect bites.

Emotional healing: In tumblestone form emerald restores the confidence of young girls and teenagers who have been teased about their weight or any young person who is made to feel inferior because parents cannot afford the latest designer goods.

Chakra: Heart.

Emeralds were considered a symbol of eternal life in Ancient Egypt. Emerald mines existed near the Red Sea coast as early as 1300 BC and were later called Cleopatra's mines because of her love of the stone. Wear or carry an emerald out of sight near your heart for attracting love, especially in later life. To call back an estranged love, speak the words you wish to say as you hold the emerald close to your lips; then seal it in an envelope and, if appropriate, send it to your love with a message.

Candle colour: *Green.*
Fragrances: *Hyssop, peach, rose.*
Practical uses: *Revives passion, whether for an interest, person or job.*
Magical significance: *To receive psychic information, place an emerald for five minutes on a Bible, then open the book at any page. The first sentences of the first page will offer the answer.*
Divinatory meaning: *You will be able to silence the sniping of someone who tries to make you feel inferior through your success.*
Zodiac: *Taurus.*
Empowerment: *I am proud of my achievements.*

Moss Agate

Type: Clear or milky white quartz that has inclusions of manganese or iron.

Colours: Either delicate green inclusions have grown into fine patterns similar to moss or lichen or the crystal is dark green with bluish inclusions that make it look like blue cheese.

Availability: Common.

Physical benefits: May assist with the relief of colds, flu and other viral illnesses and boosts immune system; improve bone marrow; assist in childbirth to reduce pain and speed delivery; speed recovery from illness; protect against low blood sugar and dehydration, pulse and heartbeat irregularities, circulation; treat fungal and skin infections; act as an anti-inflammatory.

Emotional healing: A crystal of new beginnings and the growth or regrowth of trust, releasing old fears, and reconnecting with the world after a period of disillusion.

Chakra: Heart.

Moss agate is the crystal of gardening, because planting one in a flower bed or plant pot does seem to increase the growth and health of the plant.

A helpful crystal to have near if you are struggling with tax returns, spread sheets or figures that will not add up. Keep one with bank papers to encourage savings and reverse the outflow of money.

Moss agate brings new friendships and, if worn as jewellery, will attract new love or the renewal of love. Twin moss agates kept near the bed in a green bag with dried rosemary will encourage faithful love.

Candle colour: *Dark green.*
Fragrances: *Cedarwood, juniper, moss, rosewood, rosemary, sage.*
Practical uses: *Set a moss agate beneath a pet bed or energize their water with one to help city or indoor pets to maintain connection with the natural world.*
Magical significance: *Good for connecting with fairy energies and other nature essences and for increasing the power of herbal treatments.*
Divinatory meaning: *A very lucky omen for the gradual growth of what you currently most need in your life, whether money, promotion, health or love.*
Zodiac: *Virgo.*
Empowerment: *I draw strength and harmony from the natural world.*

GREEN AGATE

Type: Chalcedony, crypto-crystalline quartz, may be infused with iron and aluminium.

Colours: Green and translucent, often banded with different greens, from mid- to darker green.

Availability: Relatively rare agate.

Physical benefits: May help with eyesight, food allergies that cause hyperactivity in children and aggressiveness in adults, and people bordering on Type 2 diabetes.

Emotional healing: An excellent stone for balancing excesses; keep tumblestones near hyperactive children and adults to deter impulsiveness.

Chakra: Heart.

Green agate is a faithful love stone, carved into a heart shape or if twin green agates are surrounded by a heart shape made out of dried rose petals. It calls slow-growing but lasting love, particularly in its darker shades; ideal to restore trust if you have been hurt previously or to bring reconciliation in an existing relationship if outsiders or family members caused a rift. Beloved by the Ancient Egyptians for seals, amulets, rings and for adorning vessels.

Candle colour: *Green.*
Fragrances: *Basil, bay, cedar, fern, moss.*
Practical uses: *A bowl of green agate tumblestones will restore the balance in any place or situation.*
Magical significance: *Buy a green agate frog if you would like twins or triplets.*
Divinatory meaning: *There are many blessings in your life and these you gladly share; make sure others are equally generous.*
Zodiac: *Virgo.*
Empowerment: *All is right in my world.*

TIBETAN TURQUOISE

Type: Hydrous aluminium phosphate coloured by copper (blue) and iron (green).

Colours: From light to deep blue (the most valuable) or greenish blue or apple green, often with spider-web black, dark grey or brown veins and streaks.

Availability: Common.

Physical benefits: May help problems with liver, anaemia and blood health, nerve endings, physical strength, mobility, ear and inner ear, eyesight, throat, bladder weakness, stomach acidity and problems, rheumatism, gout, viral infections, muscles, pain relief, cramps and as an anti-inflammatory.

Emotional healing: An excellent anti-hysteria stone, worn to calm people who over-react; helpful for narcissists who sees the world only from their point of view.

Chakra: Solar Plexus, Throat.

Candle colour: *Turquoise.*
Fragrances: *Acacia, copal, frankincense, galbanum, sandalwood.*
Practical uses: *The ultimate prosperity and luck bringer; keep turquoise in the centre of a pattern of blue and green crystals to attract good fortune and also the health to enjoy it.*
Magical significance: *Tibetan turquoise is said to absorb the essence of the owner; its colour changes with the moods and health of the owner, becoming greener or paler if the owner is sad or unwell; also transmits the health and happiness stored within it when touching your turquoise in more joyous moods.*
Divinatory meaning: *It is possible to go for a leadership position or promotion, but you may be happier fulfilling your life in other ways.*
Zodiac: *Sagittarius.*
Empowerment: *I am in good health and will remain so.*

In Tibet, turquoise is worn as jewellery and in sacred prayer beads. A turquoise rosary is said to help prayer to whatever deity is being invoked.

Tibetan turquoise is traditionally received as a gift so that it passes on its fortune-bringing powers. If you buy your own, make it a gift to yourself, a special purchase; hold it for a few minutes to transfer its good luck into your life.

Turquoise jewellery is a promise of fidelity and protection to a lover or partner. A master healing crystal that will empower other crystals, turquoise is enhanced in healing powers if set in copper or silver. Place on the Solar Plexus in the upper centre of the stomach to empower the whole body.

TSVAROVITE/TSVAROLITE GARNET

Type: Silicate/calcium aluminium silicate, transparent green variety of grossular garnet.

Colours: Pale to emerald green.

Availability: Obtainable through specialist jewellery and crystal stores and online.

Physical benefits: May help with immune system, heart and lungs, pituitary and thyroid glands, plant, animal and pollen allergies, blood-sugar disorders, skin irritation, boils, swollen scar tissue or wounds, detoxifying kidneys and blood, influenza and repeated colds, restoring libido in women; an anti-inflammatory.

Emotional healing: If people have played favourites with you since childhood or you are the family scapegoat, wearing tsavorite releases the cycle and stops you accepting the blame in every situation.

Chakra: Heart.

Candle colour: *Green.*
Fragrances: *Bluebell, galbanum, geranium, honeysuckle, mimosa.*
Practical uses: *Wear tsavorite to boost feelings of joy and positive thinking that attract abundance, in terms of improved quality of life and openness in getting to know people on the fringes of your life.*
Magical significance: *If you are unattached, every Friday, the day of Venus and love, put two small pieces of matching tsavorite in front of a lighted green candle to call love or call back lost love. Leave the candle to burn for about 20 minutes.*
Divinatory meaning: *Disapproval from someone close over a new interest or activity will lessen if you persist.*
Zodiac: *Virgo.*
Empowerment: *I will please myself this time.*

Tsavorite is the name used most frequently in the USA, tsavolite in Europe. Meditate with tsavorite to facilitate communication with higher spiritual realms. Regular use increases psychic abilities, particularly intuition.

It also releases old emotional trauma or feelings of inadequacy, assisting you to trust people and life. Green garnets reduce the power of factions at work and prevent competition between siblings in the home.

If you feel threatened by the success of others, tsavorite worn as a necklace or ring or carried near the heart helps you to recognize your own blessings and to work to attain whatever is missing.

WAVELLITE

Type: Hydrated aluminium phosphate; fibrous.

Colours: Usually green, but also white, colourless, yellow or brown.

Availability: Obtainable from specialist crystal stores and online.

Physical benefits: Believed to stimulate antibodies to resist infection and disease; said to be a good detoxifier and to ease illnesses brought on or made worse by shock or trauma.

Emotional healing: Aids bonding and healing of rifts between parents, step-parents, adoptive and foster children.

Chakra: Heart and Solar Plexus.

Wavellite is considered a magical gift from the earth spirits. Radial (wheel-like) clusters of wavellite are often found embedded in limestone or chert, reflecting light to produce a sparkling pinwheel star effect – in Native American lore stars that fell to earth that were enclosed in rock to keep them safe. Wavellite increases lucid and psychic dreams and aids dream recall. Use it in past-life healing therapy to reduce past-life trauma.

Candle colour: *Green.*
Fragrances: *Apple, rose, violet.*
Practical uses: *Use as a study aid to help you understand all aspects of a subject.*
Magical significance: *Carry wavellite during the new moon and crescent moon periods improves intuition; when held in full moonlight, it allows us to glimpse opportunities ahead.*
Divinatory meaning: *You have a decision to make that may affect your longer-term future.*
Zodiac: *Aquarius.*
Empowerment: *I will not be pressurized to make decisions before I am ready.*

ADAMITE

Type: Phosphate, arsonate.

Colours: Most commonly lime or yellow-green or yellow.

Availability: Readily obtainable from specialist crystal and mineral stores and online.Physical benefits: Said to be beneficial for heart, lungs, throat, Seasonal Affective Disorder, menstrual and hormonal problems.

Emotional healing: Good for freeing blocked communication, helps resist emotional manipulation especially by those who play on weakness or guilt.

Chakra: Heart and Throat.

Though adamite is named after the 19th-century French mineralogist Gilbert Joseph Adam, it has become associated with the quest for knowledge and the desire to regain Paradise after the fall of Adam because of its transformative fluorescent properties. For this reason, adamite will bring wealth and success through the expression of existing talents and give quiet people deserved recognition.

   WARNING: Handle with care as toxic; do not ingest, and wash your hands after handling.

Candle colour: *Green.*

Fragrances: *Lemon, lemongrass, lime, pine, wintergreen, witch hazel.*

Practical uses: *Adamite will discourage interruptions from neighbours, colleagues and distracting chatter; keep on a shelf above the phone to discourage cold callers.*

Magical significance: *Adamite is excellent when using a pendulum, tarot cards or runes to decide between options.*

Divinatory meaning: *Speak what is in your heart rather than suffering in silence.*

Zodiac: *Cancer.*

Empowerment: *I have the right to my opinions and my beliefs.*

Green Aventurine

Type: Microcrystalline quartz, sometimes containing mica that gives aventurine a metallic, iridescent glint.

Colours: Light to dark green.

Availability: Common.

Physical benefits: May benefit irregular heart rhythms, fertility, genito-urinary problems, eyesight especially long-sightedness and astigmatism, dyslexia, dyspraxia, cerebral palsy, hay fever.

Emotional healing: Leave one in the soil of a green plant overnight and hold it in the morning to let Mother Earth replace depression and anxiety with wellbeing and hope.

Chakra: Heart.

Green aventurine helps children and adults with written work, typing and computer skills, and reduces clumsiness. One of the best crystals for conceiving a baby: when you are close to ovulation, dig a small hole in earth, break an egg in the hole, place the green aventurine in the broken egg shell in the earth and fill the hole. Green aventurine increases the power of homeopathic remedies. Have green aventurine in your office or home if you live or work in a city centre.

Candle colour: *Green.*
Fragrances: *Cedarwood, rosewood, wintergreen.*
Practical uses: *The luckiest of all crystals. Keep one with you in a green bag and a four-leafed clover if you can get one, for all games of chance. Green amazonite in the same bag will increase the luck.*
Magical significance: *Green aventurine is called fairy treasure. Place three in a dish in front of your garden gnome to attract good luck to your home.*
Divinatory meaning: *Speculate to accumulate.*
Zodiac: *Virgo and Taurus.*
Empowerment: *I attract good fortune into my life.*

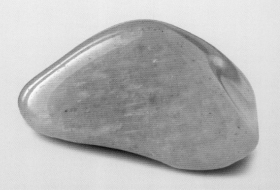

BLOODSTONE/HELIOTROPE

Type: A jasper form of chalcedony.

Colours: Dark green with red or orange spots and sometimes white markings.

Availability: Common.

Physical benefits: May be good for lower back pain, nosebleeds, blood disorders such as anaemia, diabetes, high blood pressure and circulation problems, healthy bone marrow and intestines, PMS, menstrual problems and the menopause, and for women to keep up their strength in labour.

Emotional healing: The long-term effects of bullying, mental as well as physical; helping mothers to bond after a traumatic birth or one where mother and baby were separated for a time because the baby was early.

Chakra: Root and Sacral and Heart.

Candle colour: *Red.*
Fragrances: *Copal, cinnamon, cumin, dragon's blood, ginger.*
Practical uses: *For all sports and exercise, whether you are a beginner or a professional athlete,*
Magical significance: *For helping you tune in to the power of the weather, for example winds to bring change or rain to wash away sorrow; also for recalling past lives.*
Divinatory meaning: *You can get what you want with politeness if you stand your ground and repeat your words until you are heard.*
Zodiac: *Aries.*
Empowerment: *I welcome challenges.*

"Heliotrope" means turning with the sun. Dipped in water, the stone was believed to transfer the power of the sun to cure any wound or blood disorder.

Bloodstone is helpful as a mother goddess stone for easing misunderstandings with mothers. Keep a crystal by family photographs of your mother. It also assists diets and detoxes by removing underlying emotional issues. Sew a tiny bloodstone into the lining of the coat of a child who is being bullied.

Keep a bloodstone in a glass pot of loose change where natural light shines on it to attract money to your home or business. Lucky for any sports competitions, kept in a sports bag or taped inside the programme if you are a spectator.

GREEN FLUORITE

Type: Halide, calcium fluoride.

Colours: Green.

Availability: Common.

Physical benefits: May help heals infections by boosting the immune system, regeneration of cells, energy and vitality, absorption of minerals, especially for teeth and bones, blood vessels, lungs and spleen.

Emotional healing: Green fluorite releases blocked grief from an unresolved bereavement, sometimes years earlier or in childhood, healing the freed emotions and bringing new growth; also helps with eating disorders.

Chakra: Heart.

Green as well as other coloured fluorites was carved into vessels in China more than 500 years ago and used as substitute for jade. Green fluorite offers the same beneficial energies as pure fluorite but adds growth and nature energies to bring a breath of fresh air to the most polluted setting. Give a piece to children who travel through fume-filled streets to school or have to play in urban areas. If you love butterflies, keep a piece of green fluorite in your garden to attract them.

Candle colour: *Green.*
Cragrances: *Balm of Gilead, eucalyptus.*
Practical uses: *Keep green fluorite in a room where children play to minimize conflict.*
Magical significance: *Use a green fluorite wand to programme other crystals for healing purposes. Touch with the wand and state the name of the person to be healed.*
Divinatory meaning: *Beware of mistaking sentiment and extravagant expression of devotion for true caring*
Zodiac: *Pisces*
Empowerment: *I will not be swayed by false sentiment.*

BUDDSTONE

Type: Called African or Transvaal jade, in fact a form of grossular garnet but resembles jade.

Colours: Rich deep green or sometimes lighter and mottled.

Availability: From specialist mineral stores and online.

Physical benefits: Said to help headaches, migraines, pain relief, toxicity, menstruation, muscles, kidneys, bladder, stress incontinence, genital diseases/infections, diabetes, hypoglycaemia, dizziness, Alzheimer's disease, senile dementia.

Emotional healing: For those caring for small children, disabled family members, terminally ill or elderly confused relatives to develop patience and stamina.

Chakra: Heart.

Buddstone (also known as Transvaal Jade) comes from Zimbabwe and Transvaal in South Africa, and is opaque like jade but has more active energies. It encourages step-by-step growth and is good for foot complaints; helps to make non-confrontational, determined progress against corruption or tough odds while inducing a sense of wellbeing and certainty that all will be well. Buddstone in the bedroom reduces sleep disturbances and nightmares. Pass over and round the body regularly to remove negativity and create a shield. It also encourages self-sufficiency of all kinds.

Candle colour: *Deep rich green.*
Fragrances: *Fennel, hyacinth, lavender, lilac, rosemary.*
Practical uses: *Place at the four outermost compass points downstairs in the home and a fifth in the centre to harmonize and energize.*
Magical significance: *A talisman to draw the beauty, strength and courage of African creatures into your life.*
Divinatory meaning: *A chance to put right past resentment and talk amicably with a former rival or enemy.*
Zodiac: *Virgo.*
Empowerment: *I can free myself from the inner voices of doubt.*

RUBY IN ZOISITE/ANYOLITE

Type: Epidote (calcium aluminium silicate) with ruby (corundum) inclusions.

Colours: Green, dark pink to red and black.

Availability: Relatively common as tumblestones.

Physical benefits: Claimed to assist with reproductive disorders, especially fibroids and fertility problems; bring healing after a miscarriage or termination, a hysterectomy or early menopause; slow down racing pulse and heartbeat; protect against viruses and infections, especially ones bacterial in nature.

Emotional healing: Good for worries over sexual dilemmas.

Chakra: Crown, Heart and Solar Plexus.

Ruby in zoisite or anyolite is a beautiful combination of red ruby crystals in green zoisite, merging the energies of fire and earth, passion and patience, immediacy and allowing life to unfold. It gives us the strength of mind to pursue our dreams while still keeping us connected with the real world and balancing our own needs with those of others. Good for helping children and teenagers to understand that they have to keep necessary rules and laws without feeling over-controlled or resentful. This crystal calms swings of mood and over-reaction; good for cooling the emotional and sexual temperature at work and in social situations where a liaison would be unwise or inappropriate.

Candle colour: *Green or red.*
Fragrances: *Apple and apple blossom, ginger, jasmine, magnolia.*
Practical uses: *Keep this crystal near your bed to restore passion and heal relationship issues if one partner is having sexual difficulties or is contemplating infidelity.*
Magical significance: *Use ruby in zoisite in Mars and Venus sacred sex rituals or Tantric sex where lovemaking becomes a spiritual expression of unity.*
Divinatory meaning: *A time for balancing your desire for immediate action with the safer but duller path of waiting and seeing.*
Zodiac: *Aries and Taurus.*
Empowerment: *I acknowledge the need to balance passion with practicality.*

MOOKAITE

Type: Silicate; contains chert, sometimes with fossilized inclusions.

Colours: Mottled.

Availability: Increasingly common.

Physical benefits: Thought to boost immune system, calms digestive system by reducing stress, bladder, cystitis, blood sugar disorders (high), cuts, wounds, fluid retention, bloating, hernia, thyroid.

Emotional healing: Makes it easier to accept change and to allow ourselves to take a chance now and then, without worrying about the future.

Chakra: Root, Sacral and Solar Plexus.

Mookaite is a form of jasper found in Western Australia, and is named after the district where it is mined. An Australian Aboriginal Mother Earth stone that is becoming increasingly popular throughout the world for healing and connecting with positive earth energies, even in cities.

 A very protective and grounding stone, whilst at the same time providing a motivational energy boost. For those who feel a bit stuck in either their personal life or at work, this gem can bring about the courage to seek adventure.

Candle colour: *Pink.*
Fragrances: *Basil, bay, patchouli, sage, vetivert.*
Practical uses: *Use mookaite when you need to make a decision and there are conflicting factors to consider – hold it close to receive a gut answer and go with it, even if external circumstances suggest otherwise.*
Magical significance: *As a Mother Earth stone, mookaite connects you with earth power; press a palm stone against your upper stomach.*
Divinatory meaning: *An adventurous and challenging time ahead.*
Zodiac: *Virgo and Scorpio.*
Empowerment: *Beauty is everywhere if I stop and look.*

Amegreen

Type: Amethyst and chlorite or prasiolite (natural green amethyst)

Colours: Mauve/purple and green.

Availability: Obtainable from specialist crystal stores and online, but becoming rarer.

Physical benefits: May help hearing difficulties and ear infections, sleep disturbances and disorders such as narcolepsy, snoring and apnoea, heart disease and recovery from injury, accident or trauma.

Emotional healing: A crystal for those who love too much or give too much to others, to draw boundaries and to ask for and accept support from others.

Chakra: Heart, Brow and Crown.

A very spiritual crystal that offers instant links with your guardian angel, especially outdoors; if worn or carried, automatically cleanses the aura psychic energy field and the chakra inner psychic energy centres. Use for spiritual healing of self and others, held in the hand you do not write with and circle anti-clockwise close to the skin near a site of pain or close to the heart to draw out illness or sorrow; a crystal of small miracles when nothing seems to be working health-wise or in life.

Candle colour: *Purple or green.*
Fragrances: *Benzoin, peppermint.*
Practical uses: *A natural money maker, whether in business or through personal ventures, amegreen can act as a money magnet, but make sure air can circulate all round it.*
Magical significance: *Very powerful against psychic or psychological attack.*
Divinatory meaning: *Your spiritual powers are developing fast and you will soon have a chance to use them in the way that is right for you.*
Zodiac: *Pisces.*
Empowerment: *I trust my spiritual abilities to guide me on the right path.*

GYROLITE

Type: Phyllosilicate, hydrated calcium silicate hydroxide.

Colours: White, colourless, green and brown.

Availability: Obtainable from specialist mineral stores and online.

Physical benefits: Gyrolite is claimed to bring balance to the body, especially the spine and the skeletal system.

Emotional healing: Reduces excessive introspection and introversion where people shut themselves away from company; removes the secrecy from addictions and so makes them more amenable to treatment.

Chakra: Root.

Gyrolite is a balancing mineral in every aspect of life as well as within the body and mind; keep a small piece in a cloth bag with you if you have a hectic day ahead. As a meditation crystal, it connects with ancient wisdom; whatever your field of expertise you may afterwards find you know new information without consciously learning it. A crystal of quiet strength, have it near when you need to say no; good for the willpower to stick to rules you established; if teenagers are pressurizing you to go to places you are uncertain about, touch your gyrolite, take a deep breath and refuse to be moved.

Candle colour: *Brown.*
Fragrances: *Fennel, fern, lavender, lemon verbena, neroli.*
Practical uses: *An excellent crystal for people who are shy.*
Magical significance: *Empowers other crystals; keep some with your healing crystal set.*
Divinatory meaning: *Avoid allowing others to involve you in a crisis they have exaggerated out of all proportion.*
Zodiac: *Virgo.*
Empowerment: *There is nothing to worry about.*

AGATIZED CORAL

Type: Formed when ancient lime-based coral is gradually replaced by agate (chalcedony).

Colours: From white and pink to golden yellow, with small flower-like patterns in the agate.

Availability: Obtainable from specialized crystal stores or online.

Physical benefits: May assist breathing difficulties, also diseases such as bone weakness, such as brittle bone disease or osteoporosis; believed to be protective against falls and bone fractures, especially in children and older people.

Emotional healing: Eases personality disorders, outbursts of temper, gambling, drinking addiction to sex or clairvoyant phone lines.

Chakra: Sacral and Root.

Candle colour: *Cream.*

Fragrances: *Eucalyptus, sweetgrass.*

Practical uses: *Reduces over-sensitivity to the environment when taking small children into noisy places.*

Magical significance: *Empower a piece to bring you ease in difficult social situations: hold between your hands while saying nine times, "Make me shine like the sun and flow like the waters." Repeat.*

Divinatory meaning: *A gentle response towards a difficult person will produce good results within a short time.*

Zodiac: *Cancer.*

Empowerment: *I can transform my life and still preserve what I value.*

Agatized fossil corals occur in many parts of the world and may be up to 395 million years old. One kept in a teenager's bedroom or given as earrings will help to filter over-loud music, especially through headphones, that can damage hearing.

Agatized coral increases imagination and is the stone of fiction writers, transmitting ideas while preserving integrity. If you belong to a dysfunctional family, agatized coral replaces obsession or old wounds with harmony and the ability to mend the spirit and move forward.

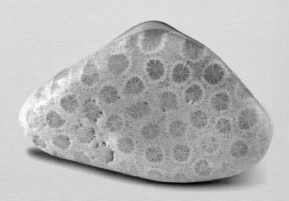

Uvite

Type: Silicate (tourmaline group).

Colours: Yellow-brown, light to dark brown, dark green to black.

Availability: Once rare, but now more common.

Physical benefits: May help with immune system, digestive disorders; be helpful after a colostomy or ileostomy, stomach stapling or gastric-band surgery, useful for fertility and male potency.

Emotional healing: Boosts self-confidence where a person has been undermined over a number of years, perhaps as the youngest child in a family.

Chakra: Heart, Root and Solar Plexus.

Uvite is a member of the tourmaline group of minerals named after the Uva district in Sri Lanka and is magnesium- and iron-rich. The difference between the other tourmalines, such as dravite, schorl or elbaite and uvite is that one of the aluminium elements has been replaced by magnesium. It has stubby crystals rather than the normal longer prismatic typical tourmaline crystals. Uvite offers grounding energies to make you feel secure within yourself.

Candle colour: *Any earthy colour.*
Fragrances: *Coriander, dragon's blood.*
Practical uses: *The ultimate environmental crystal; assists any form of green activity.*
Magical significance: *Used in earth healing rituals and those to awaken personal responsibility for global warming.*
Divinatory meaning: *Do not allow someone with a lot of money to intimidate you.*
Zodiac: *Aries and Scorpio.*
Empowerment: *I am content with what I have.*

CAT'S EYE

Type: Varies according to the crystal or gem; officially only chrysoberyl is referred to as cat's eye, others are called, for example, ruby cat's eye in the jewellery trade.

Colours: Varies according to the crystal or gem but always displays the effect of a moving cat's eye.

Availability: Relatively common as the less valuable or occidental cat's eye quartz. More exotic chrysoberyl is often called oriental cat's eye.

Physical benefits: Tought to be helpful for eyesight, coughs, haemorrhoids, hair and skin health, mobility, nausea, cholesterol, blood sugar fluctuations.

Emotional healing: Use if you are easily influenced by others

Chakra: Heart.

Candle colour: *Green.*
Fragrances: *Apple blossom, catmint, cedar, lilac, sandalwood.*
Practical uses: *Cat's eye helps you to remember where you left things; also good for all forms of speculation where you assess odds.*
Magical significance: *Considered in India as a lucky charm against sorrow, poverty, diseases and hidden enemies.*
Divinatory meaning: *Distinguish between loyal friends and superficial ones.*
Zodiac: *Pisces.*
Empowerment: *I do not need to accept unpleasant behaviour in others.*

As light hits tiny tube-like cavities or needle-like fibres within the gem or crystal, if the cavities or fibre bundles lie in the same direction, a single band of light bounces off at right angles creating the cat's eye effect.
  Cat's eyes in the Near and Middle East are considered protective against the evil eye, to make the wearer invisible and to attract wealth. Any jewellery therefore is incredibly lucky financially, as well as protective against malice and envy. People often wear the same cat's eye for years so it grows in strength and good fortune; traditionally bought on Wednesday, Thursday or Friday.

RUTILATED QUARTZ

Type: Silicate/nesosilicate, rutiles or oxide crystal needles within quartz.

Colours: Gold, silver, can be reddish to deep red.

Availability: Common.

Physical benefits: Reported as useful for bronchitis and asthma, regenerating brain cells, improving the condition of blood vessels and veins, transplants and transfusions. Emotional healing: For anyone who has dabbled unwisely in black magic.

Chakra: Root and Crown.

Various names have been given in different traditions to describe what appears to be golden hair within this crystal, for example angel hair, and rutilated quartz is an excellent angel communication crystal. It is also called the golden hair of the Roman love goddess Venus or the Viking goddess of beauty Freya; the goddesses' golden hair was preserved by the earth spirits when it was cut, because they could not bear to see it thrown away.

Candle colour: *Gold.*
Fragrances: *Cinnamon, copal, sage.*
Practical uses: *One of the best crystals for bringing out talent, particularly in the areas of creative crafts and performing in public.*
Magical significance: *Each is thought to contain a guardian spirit who will protect the owner or user from harm.*
Divinatory meaning: *Why not try for that elusive bid for fame? The energies are right and you are far more talented than you realize.*
Zodiac: *Leo.*
Empowerment: *It is never too late to follow a dream.*

CRYSTAL ANGELS

Type: Crystal angels – polished crystals carved into angel shapes, some as pendants – come in many crystal kinds and sizes; read the separate crystal entries to choose the one that is right for you.

Colours: Varies according to crystal kind.

Availability: Common from gift shops, crystal stores and online.

Physical healing: Crystal angels amplify the power of the crystal type; they are said to help when the cause of an illness cannot be discovered or the patient is resistant to treatment, for major surgery or when treatment is prolonged.

Emotional healing: Use for channelling healing from the angels; also for pregnant women, newborn babies, children or teenagers who feel vulnerable or afraid.

Chakra: Brow and Crown.

Buy a variety of crystal angels, as the form amplifies the healing, protective and spiritual properties of any crystal. If you have a challenge at work, at home or in love, choose an angel by passing your hand or a pendulum over each of the angels in turn and you will feel the one who is most helpful.

  Make an angel place by purchasing a medium-sized clear crystal angel and setting it on a small table in the centre of your home. Add fresh flowers and a regularly light a white candle and floral incense. You will notice how harmonious and peaceful your home feels even if you have a hectic life or a large family.

Candle colour: *White. Fragrances: Lavender, lotus, rose or any floral fragrance.*

Practical uses: *Buy a birthstone or zodiac angel for a newborn baby or as a birthday gift to bring good fortune, health and happiness.*

Magical significance: *Set four crystal angels in the four main directions in a room: red jasper for Uriel who stands in the north, citrine or amethyst for Raphael in the east, clear quartz or carnelian for Michael in the south and moonstone in the west for Gabriel. Each night, touch each angel in turn.*

Divinatory meaning: *Unexpected help is at hand in a current crisis or uncertainty.*

Zodiac: *Cancer and Leo for lunar moon and solar energies combined.*

Empowerment: *I connect with my inner angel.*

DIAMOND

Type: Carbon, the hardest gem and mineral in the world.

Colours: Colourless with brilliant lustre, reflecting dazzling colour flashes known as fire; also yellow, brown, green, blue, pink, purple and black diamond – not black but with black inclusions.

Availability: Common.

Physical benefits: Diamond is a master healer because it is good for healing the mind and body; said to amplify the power of other crystals if arranged in a grid or pattern round a patient; may help detoxification, brain functioning, balance of brain hemispheres, female fertility, sexual dysfunction.

Emotional healing: Creates a sense of radiance and self-value, for anyone who has lost their identity and sense of worth.

Chakra: Crown.

Because diamonds absorb thoughts and feelings, focus on remaining positive while wearing or holding them; the diamond will amplify positivity, projecting your thoughts outwards, so attracting a positive reaction from others. Rough diamond elixir counteracts exhaustion; put a few drops in your bath to energize you; add six drops of ylang ylang essential oil to the mix, shake well before adding to the bath to fill your aura with desirability before going on a date or lovemaking. Diamonds are traditionally a stone of courage, worn next to the skin by Roman soldiers to make them invincible to fear.

Candle colour: *White.*

Fragrances: *Frankincense, lily, white lotus, white orchid, white rose.*

Practical uses: *A symbol of fidelity; becomes cloudy if love is no longer true or when the wearer is unhappy about love; a sign to talk to your partner.*

Magical significance: *A natural defence against jealousy. Wear diamond earrings or pendant to protect your Brow, Throat and Heart chakras.*

Divinatory meaning: *Proof of your abilities will come from an unexpected source.*

Zodiac: *Aries*

Empowerment: *I attract light and love.*

GENERATOR QUARTZ

Type: A natural quartz point in which six equally sized sides join sharply to form a terminating point.

Colours: Depends on quartz but usually clear quartz.

Availability: Relatively rare.

Physical benefits: Reported as benefiting all surgery, laser treatment and light therapies, radiotherapy, dentistry, conditions requiring regular injections, successful childhood and adult inoculations, relief of acute pain; as the name suggests, the crystal generates, focuses and transmits via the point concentrated energy on every level.

Emotional healing: An awakener for anyone who has lost enthusiasm, passion or the ability to take action; touch the tip to the navel to awaken physical desire and emotional needs, the centre of the upper stomach to restore enthusiasm, and the heart to reconnect with people and trust.

Chakra: Crown.

A generator crystal is a healing tool to use like a laser wand in healing grids. Touch each of the crystals set round a patient to join the crystals with visualized lines of light. You can also use it for absent healing by touching a central crystal sphere or pyramid representing a sick person or animal with the tip; then in turn touch a layout of six smaller crystals or crystal points, set round the pyramid or sphere, to create a power grid. Finally, draw visualized light lines from each of the six small crystals to connect each to the central pyramid or sphere, in order to make a star of healing light. Except in absent healing, generator crystals are too powerful for children or animals.

Candle colour: *White.*
Fragrances: *Anise, benzoin, bergamot, lemon, lemongrass.*
Practical uses: *Use your generator to bring joy to an outing. Touch a packed picnic basket or luggage before a trip, any event-entrance, travel or theatre tickets; picture yourself and anyone accompanying you having a good time.*
Magical significance: *A ready-made magic wand: to create a protective circle of light, turn round clockwise, tip pointing outwards, before you face confrontation or before travelling; for wishes touch a written wish with the tip as you say it aloud, then raise the crystal and lower it vertically to retouch the words.*
Divinatory meaning: *Health, enthusiasm and energy are returning or increasing and any plans will go well.*
Zodiac: *Sagittarius, the Archer.*
Empowerment: *I generate the power to attain what I desire.*

PHANTOM QUARTZ

Type: A quartz crystal in which a phantom or shadow crystal appears. Often the phantom quartz is a pyramid. Phantoms grow in other quartzes such as amethyst and may contain a phantom of another crystal kind such as chlorite.

Colours: Depends on the inner crystal, which may be white, green, blue, red or purple.

Availability: Relatively common.

Physical benefits: Believed to help with shadows on lungs, scans, radiation treatment, micro-surgery, illnesses for which the cause is not fully understood, psychosomatic conditions, deep vein thrombosis, old illnesses that flare up.

Emotional healing: Relieves shadows from the past that still cause sorrow; for forgiving yourself if a loved one died with bitterness between you; overcomes fears of death.

Chakra: Brow.

A phantom is caused by a pause in a crystal's growth, leaving a phantom within the crystal after it continued to grow. Sometimes quartz encloses another phantom crystal or another crystal grows around quartz that stopped growing. Red phantoms release anger and repressed power; purple phantoms or those in amethyst unblock emotions or develop spiritual potential; blue phantoms allow natural wisdom to be expressed and remove a sense of injustice from the past. The white or true ghost phantom is a talisman for any makeover or transformation after a setback. A silver phantom where tiny sparkling crystals become embedded around the phantom attracts good fortune.

Candle colour: *Grey.*
Fragrances: *Lavender, mugwort, musk, myrrh, thyme.*
Practical uses: *A phantom quartz, either white or amethyst, is a wonderful crystal for a pregnant woman. Place the phantom on the womb to connect with the unborn child. Take along to scans and the birth, and then place in the nursery so the angels said to live in phantom quartz will protect the child.*
Magical significance: *Use phantom quartz to see a presence in old places. Look through the crystal and the inner phantom if you sense a ghost; you may see in your mind the spirit, or an apparition may build up externally.*
Divinatory meaning: *Something is troubling you, a reminder that you need to clear unfinished business.*
Zodiac: *Aquarius.*
Empowerment: *I do not fear shadows from the past.*

DRAGON'S EGG

Type: Usually clear quartz.

Colours: Depends on the mineral but characterized by a polished glass-like window revealing the crystalline interior.

Availability: Obtainable from specialist crystal stores and online, worthwhile obtaining several in different minerals. Physical benefits: May aid ovaries and female reproductive system, fertility, communication difficulties in children, particularly Asperger's syndrome, Tourette's and autism.

Emotional healing: Helps children in care.

Chakra: Root and Solar Plexus.

Many dragon's egg pebbles sold have a natural frosted finish on the outside from being in streams, while others are abraded to give a rough powdery exterior. One side is cut and polished to create a crystalline window revealing the inclusions in the centre of the pebble. Ideal as a child's first crystal, particularly in the softer shades of purple amethyst and pink rose quartz; will stimulate all kinds of stories about the world within the egg; an amulet for a very sensitive child, teenager or one who has had to grow up quickly.

Candle colour: *Purple or pink.*
Fragrances: *Almond blossom, lime, tea tree.*
Practical uses: *A bowl of assorted polished pebbles act as worry stones when you are trying to get to the bottom of a matter.*
Magical significance: *Once believed to be the eggs of dragons after the baby dragon had hatched. Gaze into one and allow the markings to create images, a very portable crystal ball.*
Divinatory meaning: *A secret will be revealed if you ask the right question.*
Zodiac: *Cancer.*
Empowerment: *I look beyond the immediate to the hidden meaning.*

SOAPSTONE

Type: Concentrated form of talc, magnesium silicate; contains impurities of chloride, magnesite, dolomite and serpentine.

Colours: White, cream, green, grey, pink, green and brown.

Availability: Common.

Physical benefits: Said to aid rashes, wounds, skin ulcers, allergies affecting stomach or skin, excess fat and toxins, liver, gall bladder, digestion, hyperventilation and stress-related breathing difficulties; may balance chemical and electrical impulses, and protect against side-effects of radiotherapy.

Emotional healing: An anti-panic stone, soapstone calms those over-sensitive to atmosphere. Hold a tiny soapstone Buddha and breathe slowly till the panic subsides.

Chakra: Root.

Candle colour: *Cream.*
Fragrances: *Anise, chamomile, fern, lavender, peach.*
Practical uses: *A gentle antidote to harsh or inconsiderate behaviour, absorbing noise and hyperactivity.*
Magical significance: *In India and Africa, soapstone is traditionally used for carvings of people, animals and deities, empowered through chants and prayers; daily blessings over soapstone statues spread sacred energies.*
Divinatory meaning: *Focus on how to achieve at least part of your plans here and now.*
Zodiac: *Sagittarius.*
Empowerment: *I adapt effortlessly to the needs of the day.*

Wear soapstone (also known as steatite) jewellery to counteract radiation and electromagnetic energies at work or in the atmosphere; as earrings may be protective if you use a mobile phone a lot. Soapstone helps people with rigid ideas to adapt to a situation and acknowledge the validity of other lifestyles and beliefs.

Gentle soapstone animals and birds calm anxious or over-active children and act as guardians while they sleep. Buy a pair of soapstone animals or birds if you want a gentle, loving partner, and as many smaller creatures of the same species as you want children.

INDEX

Ailments List

AILMENT	HEALING CRYSTAL
abscesses	brown jasper p.53
abuse of all kinds	pink danburite p.25, rose quartz p.24
ADHD	charoite p.89
allergies	brown jasper p.53, citrine p.46, emerald p.99, green agate p.101, green aventurine p.106, leopardskin jasper p.63, petrified wood p.54, pink danburite p.25, poppy jasper p.35, pumice stone p.55, siderite p.58, tsvarovite garnet p.103, turquoise p.97
Alzheimer's disease	azurite p.91, buddstone p.109, cerusite p.59, milky opal p.69
anaemia	bloodstone/heliotrope p.107, poppy jasper p.35, red tiger's eye/ox eye p.37, rubellite p.38, Tibetan turquoise p.102
arthritis	cerusite p.59, copper dendrite p.43, gold p.49, lodestone p.83, turquoise p.97, white coral p.73, yellow fluorite p.47
Asperger's syndrome/autism	charoite p.89, dragon's egg p.122, lapis lazuli p.94, sugilite p.28
asthma (see also respiratory system)	emerald p.99, pink topaz p.33, rhodochrosite p.32, rutilated quartz p.117, white dolomite p.68
back (see also spine)	bloodstone/heliotrope p.107, haematite p.80, honey/amber calcite p.45, lodestone p.83, petrified wood p.54, tangerine quartz p.44
bites and stings	emerald p.99, honey/amber calcite p.45, leopardskin jasper p.63, snakeskin agate p.67
bladder/urinary system	aquamarine p.92, buddstone p.109, emerald p.99, green aventurine p.106, lemon quartz p.48, leopardskin jasper p.63, Tibetan turquoise p.102, white dolomite p.68
blisters	brown jasper p.53
bloating/fluid imbalances	aquamarine p.92, pearl p.77, white opal p.76
blood disorders	azurite p.91, banded onyx p.72, blood agate p.36, bloodstone/heliotrope p.107, haematite p.80, purple spinel p.87, red tiger's eye/ox eye p.37, snow/milky quartz p.66, Tibetan turquoise p.102, tsvarovite garnet p.103, white dolomite p.68
body odour	aquamarine p.92, magnesite p.71, sunstone p.64
boils	tsvarovite garnet p.103
bones	agatized coral p.114, banded onyx p.72, bloodstone/heliotrope p.107, cerusite p.59, clear calcite p.65, dinosaur bone p.60, green fluorite p.108, gyrolite p.113, lapis lazuli p.94, magnesite p.71, milky calcite p.74, moss agate p.100, petrified wood p.54, satin spar p.70, siderite p.58, snow/milky quartz p.66, stromatolite p.57, white coral p.73, white dolomite p.68, yellow fluorite p.47
bronchitis (see also respiratory system)	aquamarine p.92, emerald p.99, labradorite p.86, rutilated quartz p.117
bruises	pumice stone p.55, red zircon p.40
burns and scalds	morganite p.27, pink topaz p.33, sugilite p.28, white coral p.73
cell/tissue regeneration	azurite p.91, banded onyx p.72, gold p.49, green fluorite p.108, honey/amber calcite p.45, milky opal p.69, rutilated quartz p.117, snakeskin agate p.67, tanzanite p.93, white coral p.73
cerebral palsy	green aventurine p.106
chilblains	bixbite/red beryl p.34
cholesterol	astrophyllite p.61, cat's eye p.116, magnesite p.71, red aventurine p.41, yellow fluorite p.47
circulation/heart	adamite p.105, almandine garnet p.39, amegreen p.112, Andean opal p.30, azurite p.91, bixbite/red beryl p.34, black obsidian p.82, black tiger's eye p.84, blood agate p.36, bloodstone/heliotrope p.107, blue wernerite p.96, bustamite p.29, charoite p.89, cleavelandite p.75, copper dendrite p.43, emerald p.99, gold p.49, golden beryl p.51, green aventurine p.106, green fluorite p.108, haematite p.80, labradorite p.86, larvakite p.85, lodestone p.83, magnesite p.71, milky calcite p.74, molybdenite p.79, morganite p.27, moss agate p.100, pink danburite p.25, pink topaz p.33, purple spinel p.87, red aventurine p.41, rhodochrosite p.32, rose quartz p.24, rubellite p.38, ruby p.42, ruby in zoisite p.110, rutilated quartz p.117, tsvarovite garnet p.103, white dolomite p.68
coeliac disease	brown jasper p.53
constipation	brown jasper p.53, golden beryl p.51, graphite p.78
cosmetic surgery	snakeskin agate p.67, yellow fluorite p.47
cramps	ammonite p.56, charoite p.89, lodestone p.83, magnesite p.71, meteorite p.81, Tibetan turquoise p.102, white dolomite p.68
Crohn's disease	brown jasper p.53

depression	rose quartz p.24
diabetes	Andean opal p.30, bloodstone/heliotrope p.107, buddstone p.109, green agate p.101, honey/amber calcite p.45, lemon quartz p.48
diarrhoea	golden beryl p.51
digestive system	bixbite/red beryl p.34, black obsidian p.82, black tiger's eye p.84, blood agate p.36, bloodstone/heliotrope p.107, brown jasper p.53, clear calcite p.65, cobalt aura p.98, gold p.49, golden beryl p.51, golden/yellow calcite p.50, graphite p.78, honey/amber calcite p.45, leopardskin jasper p.63, magnesite p.71, meteorite p.81, pearl p.77, red zircon p.40, siderite p.58, snakeskin agate p.67, soapstone p.123, Tibetan turquoise p.102, tiger's eye p.52, uvite p.115, white coral p.73, yellow fluorite p.47
dizziness/balance	buddstone p.109, siderite p.58, turquoise p.97
dyslexia	green aventurine p.106, sugilite p.28
dyspraxia	cleavelandite p.75, green aventurine p.106
ears and hearing	amegreen p.112, blue wernerite p.96, lapis lazuli p.94, pink topaz p.33, red zircon p.40, snakeskin agate p.67, Tibetan turquoise p.102, turquoise p.97
eating disorders	blood agate p.36, morganite p.27, sugilite p.28, tiger's eye p.52
emphysema	white dolomite p.68
endocrine system	lapis lazuli p.94
energy levels	bixbite/red beryl p.34, blood agate p.36, copper dendrite p.43, golden beryl p.51, green fluorite p.108, haematite p.80, lemon quartz p.48, molybdenite p.79, poppy jasper p.35, red tiger's eye/ox eye p.37, rubellite p.38, ruby p.42, siderite p.58, tanzanite p.93, Tibetan turquoise p.102, tiger's eye p.52
epilepsy	cleavelandite p.75, emerald p.99, purple spinel p.87, tanzanite aura p.90, white coral p.73
eyes and eyesight	Andean opal p.30, cat's eye p.116, clear calcite p.65, emerald p.99, green agate p.101, green aventurine p.106, labradorite p.86, lodestone p.83, meteorite p.81, red tiger's eye/ox eye p.37, satin spar p.70, stromatolite p.57, tanzanite aura p.90, Tibetan turquoise p.102, turquoise p.97, white opal p.76
fertility	almandine garnet p.39, astrophyllite p.61, blood agate p.36, copper dendrite p.43, diamond p.119, dragon's egg p.122, emerald p.99, green aventurine p.106, honey/amber calcite p.45, milky opal p.69, pink topaz p.33, red aventurine p.41, rose quartz p.24, ruby p.42, ruby in zoisite p.110, uvite p.115, white coral p.73

fevers	emerald p.99, pink topaz p.33, snow/milky quartz p.66
fibroids	ruby in zoisite p.110
fibromyalgia	citrine p.46, red aventurine p.41, ruby p.42
fungal infections	banded onyx p.72, brown jasper p.53, moss agate p.100, red aventurine p.41
gall bladder	honey/amber calcite p.45, magnesite p.71, red zircon p.40, soapstone p.123, tiger's eye p.52
gallstones	almandine garnet p.39, golden beryl p.51
genetic diseases	ammonite p.56, dinosaur bone p.60
glandular system/hormones	adamite p.105, astrophyllite p.61, blue wernerite p.96, emerald p.99, golden beryl p.51, leopardskin jasper p.63, milky opal p.69, morganite p.27, poppy jasper p.35, satin spar p.70, sugilite p.28, tanzanite aura p.90, tsvarovite garnet p.103, white opal p.76
gout	labradorite p.86, Tibetan turquoise p.102
haemophilia	almandine garnet p.39, red aventurine p.41
haemorrhoids	cat's eye p.116
headaches	achroite tourmaline p.62, amethyst p.88, blue wernerite p.96, buddstone p.109, lapis lazuli p.94, magnesite p.71, purple spinel p.87, rose quartz p.24, stromatolite p.57, turquoise p.97
hernia	black tiger's eye p.84, red aventurine p.41
HIV/AIDS	tangerine quartz p.44
Hodgkin's lymphoma	blue wernerite p.96
Hodgkinson's disease	banded onyx p.72
hypoglycaemia	buddstone p.109
hysterectomy	blood agate p.36, ruby in zoisite p.110, snow/milky quartz p.66
immune system	almandine garnet p.39, green fluorite p.108, molybdenite p.79, moss agate p.100, rubellite p.38, ruby in zoisite p.110, sugilite p.28, tanzanite p.93, tsvarovite garnet p.103, uvite p.115, wavellite p.104
incontinence/bedwetting	buddstone p.109, citrine p.46, honey/amber calcite p.45
insomnia	charoite p.89, pink topaz p.33, red zircon p.40, white dolomite p.68
joints	brown jasper p.53, pumice stone p.55
kidneys	aquamarine p.92, brown jasper p.53, buddstone p.109, cobalt aura p.98, emerald p.99, lemon quartz p.48, tsvarovite garnet p.103, white dolomite p.68
lesions	pumice stone p.55

liver	bixbite/red beryl p.34, citrine p.46, cobalt aura p.98, golden beryl p.51, red zircon p.40, rubellite p.38, soapstone p.123, Tibetan turquoise p.102, yellow fluorite p.47
lymphatic system	aquamarine p.92, banded onyx p.72, blood agate p.36, lapis lazuli p.94
mastitis	milky opal p.69, pink chalcedony p.31
melanomas	bustamite p.29, snakeskin agate p.67
memory	citrine p.46, cleavelandite p.75, golden beryl p.51, stromatolite p.57, tanzanite aura p.90
menopause	astrophyllite p.61, bloodstone/heliotrope p.107, larvakite p.85, pink topaz p.33, ruby p.42, ruby in zoisite p.110, snow/milky quartz p.66, white dolomite p.68
menstruation	adamite p.105, almandine garnet p.39, astrophyllite p.61, blood agate p.36, bloodstone/heliotrope p.107, buddstone p.109, haematite p.80, labradorite p.86, pink tourmaline p.26, poppy jasper p.35, pumice stone p.55, red tiger's eye/ox eye p.37, rose quartz p.24, ruby p.42, satin spar p.70, white coral p.73, white dolomite p.68, white opal p.76
metabolism/ weight loss	almandine garnet p.39, clear calcite p.65, copper dendrite p.43, labradorite p.86, lemon quartz p.48, red aventurine p.41, snakeskin agate p.67, soapstone p.123, tangerine quartz p.44
migraines	amethyst p.88, buddstone p.109, lapis lazuli p.94, magnesite p.71, pink tourmaline p.26, purple spinel p.87, rhodochrosite p.32, satin spar p.70, turquoise p.97
miscarriage	ruby in zoisite p.110
mobility	bustamite p.29, cat's eye p.116, petrified wood p.54, Tibetan turquoise p.102, white coral p.73
mouth odour	aquamarine p.92
muscles	brown jasper p.53, buddstone p.109, lodestone p.83, meteorite p.81, pink danburite p.25, pumice stone p.55, rubellite p.38, snakeskin agate p.67, Tibetan turquoise p.102, white dolomite p.68
myelin sheath	cobalt aura p.98
nausea	cat's eye p.116, citrine p.46, golden beryl p.51, haematite p.80, honey/amber calcite p.45, lemon quartz p.48, pearl p.77, white coral p.73, white opal p.76
nervous system	blue wernerite p.96, gold p.49, lapis lazuli p.94, leopardskin jasper p.63, morganite p.27, pink tourmaline p.26, stromatolite p.57, tanzanite aura p.90, Tibetan turquoise p.102, white opal p.76
neuralgia	pink tourmaline p.26
nightmares	rose quartz p.24

pain	almandine garnet p.39, ammonite p.56, black obsidian p.82, buddstone p.109, dinosaur bone p.60, generator quartz p.120, haematite p.80, labradorite p.86, lapis lazuli p.94, lodestone p.83, meteorite p.81, pumice stone p.55, purple spinel p.87, red zircon p.40, sugilite p.28, Tibetan turquoise p.102
panic	pink tourmaline p.26
parasites	labradorite p.86, leopardskin jasper p.63, snakeskin agate p.67
Parkinson's disease	cerusite p.59, cleavelandite p.75, purple spinel p.87
pregnancy/ childbirth	almandine garnet p.39, ammonite p.56, banded onyx p.72, bloodstone/heliotrope p.107, citrine p.46, emerald p.99, milky opal p.69, moss agate p.100, pink chalcedony p.31, pink tourmaline p.26, pumice stone p.55, ruby p.42
prostate	black tiger's eye p.84, brown jasper p.53, cerusite p.59, sunstone p.64
psychosomatic conditions	phantom quartz p.121, red tiger's eye/ox eye p.37
reproductive system	astrophyllite p.61, banded onyx p.72, blood agate p.36, brown jasper p.53, buddstone p.109, dragon's egg p.122, green aventurine p.106, leopardskin jasper p.63, pearl p.77, pink topaz p.33, pink tourmaline p.26, red aventurine p.41, rose quartz p.24, sunstone p.64, tangerine quartz p.44, white coral p.73, white dolomite p.68
respiratory system (see also asthma; bronchitis)	adamite p.105, agatized coral p.114, aquamarine p.92, bixbite/red beryl p.34, emerald p.99, green fluorite p.108, laboradiye p.86, larvakite p.85, milky opal p.69, morganite p.27, phantom quartz p.121, pink topaz p.33, rhodochrosite p.32, rubellite p.38, soapstone p.123, tsvarovite garnet p.103, turquoise p.97, white dolomite p.68
rheumatism	cerusite p.59, copper dendrite p.43, labradorite p.86, lodestone p.83, Tibetan turquoise p.102, tiger's eye p.52, turquoise p.97, yellow fluorite p.47
scars/scar tissue	pink chalcedony p.31, pumice stone p.55, satin spar p.70, tsvarovite garnet p.103, white coral p.73
seasonal affective disorder	adamite p.105, golden beryl p.51, sunstone p.64, tangerine quartz p.44
sexual dysfunction/ potency	almandine garnet p.39, ammonite p.56, brown jasper p.53, copper dendrite p.43, diamond p.119, honey/amber calcite p.45, lodestone p.83, pearl p.77, red tiger's eye/ox eye p.37, ruby p.42, tangerine quartz p.44, tsvarovite garnet p.103, uvite p.115
shingles	yellow fluorite p.47
shock	black obsidian p.82, wavellite p.104

skin conditions	Andean opal p.30, brown jasper p.53, cat's eye p.116, citrine p.46, clear calcite p.65, labradorite p.86, larvakite p.85, lemon quartz p.48, leopardskin jasper p.63, milky opal p.69, moss agate p.100, pearl p.77, pink chalcedony p.31, poppy jasper p.35, pumice stone p.55, purple spinel p.87, red aventurine p.41, rose quartz p.24, satin spar p.70, snakeskin agate p.67, soapstone p.123, tsvarovite garnet p.103, white coral p.73
sleep	amegreen p.112, rose quartz p.24
spine	azurite p.91, gold p.49, graphite p.78, gyrolite p.113, honey/amber calcite p.45, pink tourmaline p.26, yellow fluorite p.47
spleen	cobalt aura p.98, golden beryl p.51, green fluorite p.108, honey/amber calcite p.45, rubellite p.38
sprains	tiger's eye p.52
stress-related conditions	blue jasper p.95, rhodochrosite p.32, rose quartz p.24
strokes	blue jasper p.95, cleavelandite p.75, larvakite p.85, tanzanite aura p.90
sunburn	aquamarine p.92
teeth and gums	aquamarine p.92, banded onyx p.72, blue wernerite p.96, emerald p.99, generator quartz p.120, green fluorite p.108, magnesite p.71, milky calcite p.74, molybdenite p.79, snow/milky quartz p.66, stromatolite p.57, white dolomite p.68, yellow fluorite p.47
teething	white coral p.73
tetanus	brown jasper p.53
throat	achroite tourmaline p.62, adamite p.105, aquamarine p.92, bixbite/red beryl p.34, morganite p.27, stromatolite p.57, Tibetan turquoise p.102, turquoise p.97
tongue	morganite p.27
Tourette's syndrome	dragon's egg p.122
tumours	black tiger's eye p.84, bustamite p.29, pearl p.77
ulcers	bixbite/red beryl p.34, black tiger's eye p.84, brown jasper p.53, clear calcite p.65, pumice stone p.55, soapstone p.123, sunstone p.64, tiger's eye p.52
varicose veins	brown jasper p.53
verrucas	brown jasper p.53, snakeskin agate p.67
warts	brown jasper p.53, clear calcite p.65, labradorite p.86, snakeskin agate p.67

CREDITS

Crystals on pages 1l, 1cl, 1r, 3tl, 3tcl, 3tcr, 3tr, 3bl, 3bc, 3br, 4l, 4cl, 4cr, 6, 12l, 12r, 14, 24-28, 31, 32, 34-35, 37, 41-45, 47-52, 54-66, 71-72, 75-94, 96-97, 99-100, 103-110, 112, 114-117, 119, 121-123 **courtesy of Charlie's Rock Shop**, Unit 1 The 1929 Shop, 18 Watermill Way, Merton Abbey Mills, London, SW19 2RD, tel: 020 8544 1207, fax: 020 8544 0992, website: http://www.charliesrockshop.com/

Crystals on pages 3c, 4r, 29, 30, 36, 73-74, 111, 118 **courtesy of The Crystal Healer**, http://www.thecrystalhealer.co.uk

PICTURE CREDITS SUMMARY
L=left, R=right, T=top, B=bottom.

The publishers would like to thank the following sources for their kind permission to reproduce the pictures in this book.

Alamy Images: /Blickwinkel: 101

Corbis: /Visuals Unlimited: 46, /Ric Ergenbright: 102, /Gavin Kingcome/Science Photo Library: 120

Fawcett Hobbies: 95

Gemological Institute of America: 33

Getty Images: /Scientifica: 9, 12c, 22, 67, /Alan Levenson: 20

Krystal Love: 98

Natural History Museum: 1cr, 53

Private Collection: 70

Science Photo Library: /Joel Arem: 68, 113

All other photographs copyright of Carlton Books Ltd.

Every effort has been made to acknowledge correctly and contact the source and/or copyright holder of each picture and Carlton Books Limited apologises for any unintentional errors or omissions which will be corrected in future editions of this book.